CLASSICAL INGENUITY

THE LEGACY OF GREEK AND ROMAN ARCHITECTS, ARTISTS, AND INVENTORS

by
Charles F. Baker III and Rosalie F. Baker

Dedication

In grateful appreciation to our parents, Joseph and
Rose Ferreira and Charles and Carol Baker, for their
guidance through the years.

A special note of thanks goes to Amanda Podany,
California State Polytechnic University at Pomona,
for the time she spent reviewing the text.

ABOUT THE COVER: Photograph by A.A.M. van der Heyden. Please see page 42.

Cobblestone Publishing, Inc.
7 School Street
Peterborough, NH 03458

Manufactured in the United States of America
ISBN 0-942389-07-7

All photographs by A.A.M. van der Heyden except for Comstock Inc./Georg Gerster: **13;** Scala/Art Resource,
N.Y.: **25, 89;** courtesy Charles F. Baker III: **48-49, 64-65, 67, 102;** Alinari/Art Resource, N.Y.: **62;** photo by Gary
Layda, courtesy Metro Parks, Nashville, TN: **63;** courtesy Museum of Fine Arts, Boston, Catharine Page Perkins
Fund, 95.21: **77;** The Metropolitan Museum of Art: **78 top** (Gift of El Conde de Lagunillos, 1956.56.49.1), **78 bot-
tom** (Rogers Fund, 1907.07.286.84), **78-79, 79 bottom left** (Gift of the Subscribers to the Fund for Excavations at
Sardis, 1914.14.30.26), **79 top** (Bequest of Walter C. Baker, 1971.1972.118.138), **79 bottom right** (Fletcher Fund
1931.31.11.10).

Copy-edited by Barbara Jatkola
Design by Ann C. Webster
Design Coordination by Brenda Ellis
Illustrations by Annette Cate
Maps by Coni Porter
Typesetting by Rosalie Ferreira
Printing and binding by Semline, Inc.

"Life rushes from within, not from without. There is no work of art so big or so beautiful that it was not all once contained in some youthful body."

Willa Cather (1873–1947), American novelist, *The Song of the Lark*

FOREWORD

Too often periods in history are studied as separate units that are unrelated to other periods in history. The same happens with cultures and civilizations. As a result, it is difficult for students to see how each period affects, and in many ways fosters, future events. This book aims to make students aware of the extent to which the artists, architects, and inventors of the ancient Mediterranean world have influenced their successors through the ages.

Chapter 1 introduces the Seven Wonders of the Ancient World, structures that inspired other ancients whose creations we now imitate. Chapters 2 and 4 focus on the architectural accomplishments of the ancient Greeks and Romans, while Chapter 3 features ancient artists and sculptors. All three chapters compare and contrast the two ancient cultures (Greece and Rome) and then explain how craftsmen in the Western world have imitated their predecessors. Chapter 5 focuses on the inventive genius of the Greeks.

Each chapter contains a series of puzzles that will test students' retention of the material presented. The Companion section of each chapter and the Cross Companion at the end of the book introduce questions aimed at encouraging readers to see comparisons and contrasts both in ancient times and between ancient and modern times.

A note on spelling: We have followed the Greek spelling in the transliteration of Greek names and the Latin spelling in the transliteration of Roman names. For example, Halikarnassos is spelled with a *k* and an *os* as it would have been by the Greeks. Its Latin equivalent is Halicarnassus. Exceptions: We chose to keep the *c* in Acropolis, Crete, Corinth, and Pericles and the *c* and *us* in Croesus to conform to the present-day English spelling of these names.

World of Greece and Rome

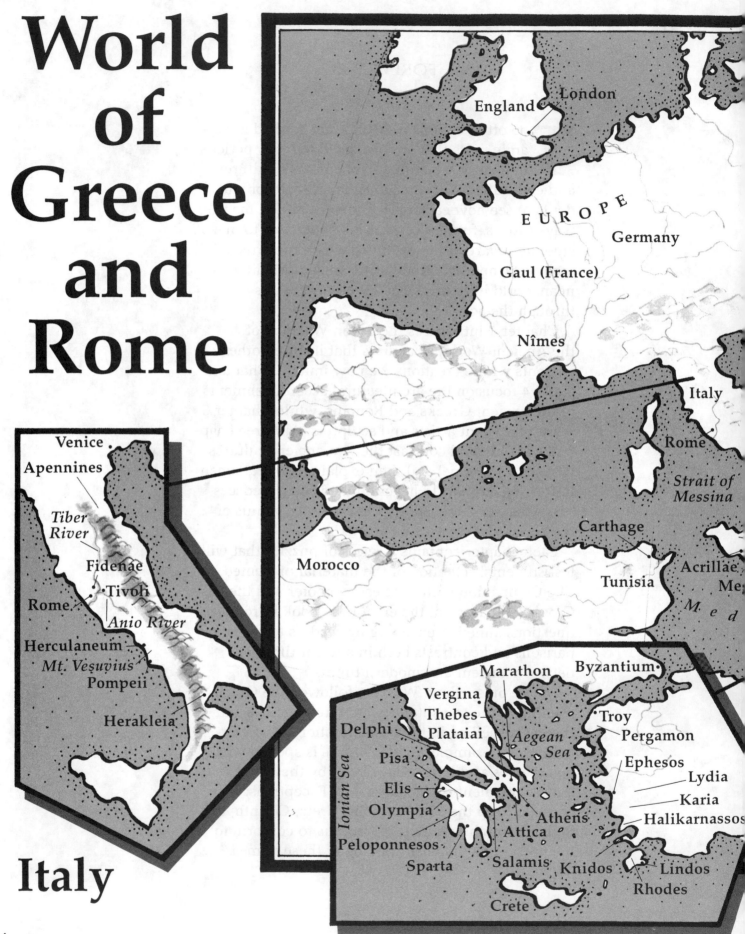

England · London

E U R O P E

Germany

Gaul (France)

Nîmes

Italy

Rome

Strait of Messina

Carthage

Morocco

Acrillae
Me

Tunisia

M e d

Italy

Venice
Apennines

Tiber River

Fidenae
·Tivoli

Rome·

Anio River

Herculaneum
Mt. Vesuvius
Pompeii

Herakleia

Marathon · Byzantium·

Vergina
Thebes·
Delphi · Plataiai · *Aegean Sea*

Troy
Pergamon

Pisa

Ephesos

Lydia

Elis

Karia

Olympia

Athens · Halikarnassos

Attica

Peloponnesos

Sparta · Salamis · Knidos · Lindos

Rhodes

Crete

Ionian Sea

6

Macedonia

Byzantium
(Constantinople, Istanbul)

Thessaly

Black Sea

Caspian
Sea

Troy

ASIA MINOR
(Turkey)

Media

Persia (Iran)

Euphrates
River

Tigris River

A S I A

Sicily
racuse

Aegean
Sea

Greece

Rhodes

Crete

Cyprus

Lebanon

Babylon

r r a n e a n   S e a

Alexandria

Pharos

Lake Mareotis

ria

Giza

Cairo

Libya

Memphis

Egypt

ARABIA

Nile River

AFRICA

Aswan

Aegean World

– maps by Coni Porter

7

"Great deeds need great preparations."

Heliodoros, third-century A.D. Greek writer

THE SEVEN WONDERS OF THE ANCIENT WORLD

THE GREAT PYRAMID OF KHUFU

The largest of three pyramids constructed around 2500 B.C. by kings of Egypt, the Great Pyramid of the pharaoh Khufu (called Cheops by the Greeks) is located at Giza on the West Bank of the Nile River. Although most of the stones were taken from nearby quarries, some came from across the Nile and other, more distant quarries.

The workers used no machinery or iron tools, only copper chisels and saws, to cut the huge limestone blocks. Thousands of other workers, their bent backs glistening with sweat under the hot Egyptian sun, dragged the blocks to the site at Giza. After the first layer of stones was in place, the workers built ramps of earth and bricks and dragged the stones up the ramps to form the next layer. As they completed each layer, they raised and lengthened the ramps, until finally the last stone was in place.

This entire mass, which covers 13 acres, contains approximately 2.3 million blocks of limestone, each weighing about 2 1/2 tons (5,000 pounds). When the outer coat of gleaming white casing stone was still intact, the pyramid reached a height of 481 feet.

Near the Great Pyramid at Giza, the Great Sphinx, built during the reign of Khufu's son Khafre (c. 2575–c. 2465 B.C.), has come to represent the Egypt of the pharaohs. The symbol of ancient Egyptian royalty, the sphinx took the form of a crouching lion with paws outstretched. Its head was a portrait statue of the king responsible for its construction.

When Herodotos, a fifth-century B.C. Greek historian, visited the Great Pyramid two thousand years later, he wrote:

The causeway, the works on the mound where the pyramid stands, and the underground burial chambers took ten years to build. The pyramid took twenty years. Square at the base and with a height equal to the length of each side, the pyramid is of polished stone blocks beautifully fitted together. Not one of the blocks is less than thirty feet long. A canal was made from the Nile, the water from which turned the site into an island.

Herodotos also commented that such a massive structure could have been built only by slave labor:

Some Egyptians were forced to drag blocks of stone from the quarries in the Arabian hills to the Nile. The blocks were then ferried across and taken over by other laborers, who hauled them to the Libyan hills. The work continued in three-month shifts, a hundred thousand men to a shift. It took ten years of this oppressive labor to build the track along which the blocks were hauled—a work, in my opinion, of hardly less magnitude than the pyramid itself.

The three-month shifts that Herodotos mentions took place during the time that the Nile River flooded its banks,[1] fertilizing the surrounding land but preventing any agricultural work from being done. During these months, many Egyptians were free to work on the royal tombs.

The Egyptian belief that an individual's body had to be preserved and protected so that the soul could live forever was the driving force behind the tombs. The Egyptians not only built colossal stone structures to shelter and protect the bodies of their pharaohs, but they also developed great skill at embalming corpses. Through the centuries, archaeologists and historians have uncovered countless mummified remains of humans and animals.

PHILON'S LIST OF WONDERS

During the second century B.C., an advanced student of applied mechanics named Philon wrote a much-celebrated work titled *The Seven Wonders of the World.* As he was a native of the Greek city of Byzantium,[1] historians refer to him as Philon of Byzantium. His list of engineering marvels, although different in some cases from those mentioned by other ancient writers, became the accepted wonders of later generations. Philon's wonders included the Great Pyramid in Egypt, the Hanging Gardens of Babylon, the temple of Artemis at Ephesos, the statue of Zeus at Olympia, the Mausoleum at Halikarnassos, the Colossos of Rhodes, and the lighthouse on the island of Pharos.

In recognition of the outstanding engineering capabilities of the ancients, in this chapter we focus on Philon's seven wonders.

1. When the Roman emperor Constantine made Byzantium the new capital of the Roman Empire, he changed the name of the city to Constantinople. Today it is known as Istanbul, a principal city of Turkey.

1. Since the completion of the Aswan High Dam in 1970, the annual flooding of the Nile has been controlled mechanically.

KHUFU'S BOAT

Entombed with Khufu's body were treasures of gold and precious objects that filled the chambers with the wealth he would need in the hereafter. Also buried with Khufu was a 141-foot boat made from the cedars of Lebanon (wood so strong that it resisted even the worm borers of the Nile River) and steered with 26-foot oars. This vessel was to provide Khufu with transportation for his voyage through eternity. Before being buried in a special airtight pit beside the pyramid, the vessel was dismantled and the 1,224 pieces were marked with shipwrights' instructions for reassembly. Today the 4,000-year-old reassembled boat stands in a museum next to the Great Pyramid.

In 1954, a young architect-archaeologist named Kamal el-Mallakh (standing next to the reconstructed boat) was the project director of a road being built near the Great Pyramid. Convinced that the irregular placement of the southern boundary wall of the pyramid meant a possible burial site, he persuaded others to begin excavating the site. Their find was Khufu's boat.

Even the pyramid shape had a religious meaning. The Egyptians thought that the sloping sides were like the slanting rays of the sun and would help the king's soul as it climbed to the sky and life among the gods in the hereafter.

Inside the Great Pyramid, a passageway leads from an entrance on one side of the structure to several rooms within. The room originally planned as the pharaoh's burial chamber became the Queen's Chamber, although no queen was buried there. Khufu had the King's Chamber constructed at the end of a corridor 153 feet long and 28 feet high. Called the Grand Gallery, this corridor is considered by many to be one of the great feats of ancient architecture.

Unfortunately, ancient Egyptian tomb robbers ravaged the Great Pyramid centuries after Khufu's death. They stole the treasures of the mighty pharaoh and even his sacred, mummified body. As the years passed, most of the white outer casing stone was stripped from the sides of the Great Pyramid and used in the construction of other tombs and temples. Still, the pyramid at Giza remains a monument to the skill and devotion of an ancient people whose extraordinary achievement has been admired throughout the ages.

Babylon is best remembered for the artfully designed gardens that towered above the city. Although no remains of these gardens have been found, according to tradition, Nebuchadrezzar II, king of Babylon (605–562 B.C.), had the gardens built to please his queen, who was homesick for the cool, mountainous land of her birth, the kingdom of Media (an ancient country located in present-day northwestern Iran). These gardens were not actually "hanging" gardens but overhanging balconies, or terraces, that were part of a roof garden that soared high above the city.

THE HANGING GARDENS OF BABYLON

The approximately three-hundred-fifty-foot-high structure comprised huge terraces planted with tier after tier of trees, shrubs, and flowers set above an enormous vaulted superstructure. In the first century B.C., the Greek historian Diodoros wrote that "the garden was four hundred feet square and surrounded by battlements and bulwarks. The ascent was similar to that which goes to the top of a mountain.... Under the steps of the ascent were arches, one above the another, rising gently by degrees. These arches supported the entire plantation. The arch upon which the platform was laid was an incredible eighty feet high."

Diodoros also noted that the base of the garden

Although archaeologists have not yet uncovered any traces of the Hanging Gardens, remains of foundation chambers and vaults that could have supported pumps and other equipment necessary to supply the water for such a garden have been uncovered in what was ancient Babylon's palace.

13

BABYLON

Babylon was once the most splendid city of the ancient East. Approximately two thousand years before the birth of Christ, Babylon was the capital of Hammurabi, the great conqueror and lawgiver. Hundreds of years later, Babylon rose to glory under King Nebuchadrezzar II, who rebuilt the city and extended its mighty fortifications. Many ancients considered the massive walls that surrounded the city as one of the wonders of the world. When the Greek writer and traveler Herodotos visited Babylon in about 450 B.C., he claimed that the walls were fifty-five miles long, eighty feet thick, and three hundred twenty feet high—walls upon which a four-horse chariot could turn.

was made of huge stones covered with reeds, asphalt, and a layer of tiles. These layers were covered with sheets of lead, which prevented the moisture that seeped through the top layer of earth from rotting the foundation.

Quintus Curtius, a Roman traveler in the first century A.D., described trees twelve feet in circumference and fifty feet high shading the gardens: "The ascent to the highest story of the gardens is by stairs, and at their side are water engines, by means of which workers, appointed expressly for the purpose, are continually employed in raising water from the Euphrates River which flows through Babylon into the gardens." Water then fell over the vegetation and dripped in front of windows, creating cool rooms within—an ancient form of air conditioning.

Building this architectural wonder was no easy task. The stones that supported the enormous weight of the earth needed for the gardens had to be hauled from great distances. Building materials were usually manmade bricks and tiles.

In the fifth century B.C., Babylon was conquered by the Persian king Cyrus. Although accounts of the conquest differ, one writer stated that Cyrus was aided by traitors from within the massive walls surrounding Babylon, the most protected city of the ancient world. According to Herodotos, Cyrus diverted the waters of the Euphrates River so that his soldiers could enter the city along the riverbed. Whatever the actual story may be, Babylon's walls and its towering gardens gradually deteriorated.

Ⓘn the fifth-century B.C. city-state of Elis, in the
northwestern corner of the Greek peninsula
known as the Peloponnesos, a temple was erected
to house a statue of Zeus, the mightiest of all the
Greek gods. In ancient times, wor-
shipers from every district in Greece
traveled to this area and the nearby
plain of Olympia every four years to
pay special tribute to Zeus in a contest
of sports. A truce was proclaimed
throughout the Greek world so that
friend and enemy alike could journey
safely to the events, known collectively
as the Olympic Games, and to worship
at the shrine of Zeus.

THE STATUE OF ZEUS AT OLYMPIA

The great temple at the site was designed by the
architect Libon of Elis. It was built on a high platform, with thirteen large columns along each side
and six on each end supporting a roof of gleaming
white marble. Detailed sculptures covered most of
the building's exterior. The eastern pediment (a low-
pitched triangular section) above the front entrance
showed a quiet scene from the Greek tale of Pelops, a
legendary king of Asia Minor, and Oenomaos, a king
who ruled over the Greek cities of Elis and Pisa. The
western pediment over the rear entrance depicted a
scene from the battle between the Centaurs (crea-
tures that are half-man, half-horse) and the Lapiths
(a mythical mountain tribe of northern Greece).

The crowning achievement, however, was the statue of Zeus within, which was created by the greatest
Greek sculptor, Pheidias of Athens. Six hundred years
later, the well-known Greek geographer and traveler
Pausanias visited the area and told of the divine statue seated on a majestic throne. Resting on a stone
pedestal three feet high and twenty-two feet wide,
the statue rose to a height of nearly forty feet and
occupied a large part of the temple's central aisle.
Pausanias also wrote in *A Guide to Greece* that,
according to tradition, when the statue was finished,
Pheidias prayed to Zeus to make a sign if the work
pleased him, and immediately a flash of lightning
struck the pavement at the very spot where a bronze
urn still stood in Pausanias's time.

Fashioned by Pheidias and his attendants in a workshop near the temple,[1] the statue was made of chryselephantine (ivory and plates of gold fastened to a wooden framework). To prevent the ivory from cracking in Olympia's damp climate, the statue was treated with oil kept in a pool in the temple floor. The throne was made of cedar covered with gold and inlaid with ebony, ivory, and precious stones. On the legs of the throne were figures of Nike, the Greek goddess of victory. The arms were formed by sphinxes clutching their Theban victims.[2] The slaughter of Niobe's family by two of Zeus's children, Apollo and Artemis,[3] was represented along the edge of the seat. On the back of the throne were the Graces[4] and the Horae.[5]

Zeus was depicted with his uplifted right hand holding a gold and ivory figurine of Nike. In his left hand was a scepter inlaid with precious metals and supporting an eagle. Eyes of brilliant stones shone forth from a face of ivory framed with wavy hair and a beard of solid gold. Zeus's feet, clad in sandals of gold, rested on a footstool, which was guarded by two golden lions. On the front of the stool was a representation of the battle between the Greek hero Theseus and the fearless nation of female warriors known as the Amazons. A mantle, also of gold and decorated with animals and flowers, flowed across Zeus's ivory shoulders.

The great beauty of this wonder of the ancient world not only increased the Greeks' devotion to Zeus as king of the gods but also added another aspect to his power over mortals: It brought peace to the minds of troubled men. Sometime during the fifth century A.D., approximately one thousand years after its construction, the statue of Zeus at Olympia was destroyed.

---

1. The remains of Pheidias's workshop were discovered in the 1950s.

2. On a rock near the entrance to the Greek city-state of Thebes sat a sphinx, a creature with the body of a winged lion and the breast and head of a maiden. The sphinx asked every passer-by the same riddle: "What walks on four legs in the morning, two at noon, and three in the evening?" If the person answered incorrectly, the sphinx flung him or her from the rock. When the Greek king Oedipus answered "a human being," the sphinx flung herself from the rock.

3. Because the mortal Niobe had dared to compare her family to that of the immortal Leto, the mother of the twin deities Apollo and Artemis, Niobe and her family were punished with death.

4. The Graces were the goddesses of grace, charm, and beauty.

5. The Horae were the goddesses of order in nature and the seasons.

In 353 B.C., Mausolos, king of Karia, an area bordering the Aegean Sea in southwestern Asia Minor (present-day Turkey), died. With no heirs to succeed him, his wife, Artemisia (a derivative of Artemis, the name of the Greek goddess of the hunt), became the next ruler of Karia. As it was the custom for the rulers of this kingdom to marry their own sisters, Artemisia also was Mausolos's sister.

The grief-stricken Artemisia resolved to honor her dead husband with a magnificent tomb. She sent emissaries to Greece to find the finest architects, sculptors, and craftsmen and invite them to Halikarnassos, the city that Mausolos had built as his capital.

Few could resist the challenge to design and construct the most splendid tomb humans or gods had ever seen. Renowned architects such as Satyros and Pythios and sculptors such as Skopas, Timotheos, Bryaxis, and Leochares sailed from Greece across the Aegean Sea to Halikarnassos at the bidding of Artemisia. Their goal was to create a monument that would be known for the beauty of its design, the richness of its sculptures, and its superb craftsmanship.

Unfortunately, Queen Artemisia died in 351 B.C., before the tomb was completed. The artists, however, were so devoted to their work that they chose to stay and finish it. The first-century A.D. Roman historian Pliny the Elder wrote that the sculptors remained "for their own fame and a record of their skill." And so there rose above the city of Halikarnassos a monument to Artemisia as well as to her husband.

The Mausoleum soared one hundred forty feet above a large rectangular courtyard. In the center, a high stone platform was accessible by a flight of marble stairs guarded by majestic sculptured lions. A second platform was enclosed by a wall on which there were sculptured standing figures of gods and goddesses. At each corner were statues of warriors on prancing horses.

Rising from this platform was the rectangular

THE MAUSOLEUM AT HALIKARNASSOS

marble tomb in which the bodies of Mausolos and Artemisia lay. The base of the chamber was decorated with sculptured reliefs, and above it rose thirty-six Ionic columns made of marble, nine to a side, supporting a pyramid of twenty-four steps that seemed to be suspended in midair. Crowning the flat-topped pyramid was a marble chariot drawn by four enormous horses, with the standing figures of Mausolos and Artemisia as passengers.

Three sculptured friezes around the lower part of the Mausoleum depicted battling Greeks and Amazons, Centaurs fighting Lapiths, and an intense chariot race. Every scene portrayed a sense of restless movement. The sun's rays reflected on the structure's glistening white marble and on the statues and friezes painted in the Greek fashion: Flesh was colored red; draperies were gold, blue, green, and white; and the warriors' weapons and the trappings of their horses were of gleaming gilt bronze.

This wonder of the ancient world survived for more than fifteen hundred years, witnessing the arrival of Alexander the Great, the dominance of Rome, the attacks of pirates, and the alternating invasions of the Crusaders and the Turks. At the beginning of the fifteenth century, earthquakes shattered the columns of the Mausoleum and sent the pyramid, with its chariot, riders, and horses, crashing down. Many marble blocks were carried off to be ground into powder to provide lime for plastering. Fortunately, some sculptures were not destroyed and eventually were preserved in museums.

Although Artemisia's monument to her husband no longer stands in its stately glory overlooking the city of Halikarnassos, Mausolos is still honored today, for his name has passed into contemporary usage in the term "mausoleum," meaning any magnificent tomb.

THE TEMPLE OF ARTEMIS AT EPHESOS

The temple of Artemis at Ephesos, a city on the west coast of Asia Minor (present-day Turkey), was larger and more splendid than the famed Parthenon in Athens, Greece. The second-century Greek traveler and geographer Pausanias observed that "it surpassed every structure raised by human hands."

The first of five shrines erected on this site for the worship of the ancient mother goddess of Asia[1] was a primitive tree shrine built in approximately 800 B.C. In 700 B.C., a stone building was constructed over and around it. This shrine was destroyed in 660 B.C. by invading European tribes. The structure was rebuilt, only to be destroyed again and replaced in 600 B.C. by a third temple of fine limestone with a porch of two columns facing west.

As Ephesos was one of the most prosperous cities in Asia Minor, its citizens were determined to rebuild the deteriorating shrine on a more magnificent scale. Neighboring states aided the Ephesians, with Croesus, the rich king of Lydia in Asia Minor, contributing most of the columns. The new temple, constructed of white marble and surrounded by Ionic columns, was four times the size of its predecessor. Years later, in 356 B.C., a young Ephesian named Herostratos burned down this temple in an attempt to make a name for himself.

Again the citizens of Ephesos began the process of rebuilding. Out of respect for Artemis, various kings presented columns for the new temple, and the women of Ephesos sold their jewels to raise funds. The Macedonian ruler Alexander the Great offered to pay the cost of the reconstruction if the Ephesians would let him dedicate the monument in his name. The Ephesians tactfully declined this

---

1. The Greek Artemis and the Asiatic mother goddess Artemis were not the same. The Greek colonists who settled in the area and later the Roman conquerors so closely identified their Artemis (the Roman Diana) with the Artemis of the Ephesians that the Greek and Roman deities adopted many characteristics of the Ephesian goddess. One belief that did not change was the idea that the Ephesian Artemis was a mother goddess, symbolized by her egglike breasts, whereas the Greek Artemis and the Roman Diana were represented as maiden goddesses who roamed the woods, not the homes and cities built by people.

offer by replying that one god could not dedicate a temple to another.

The temple was finished in 323 B.C. It measured 425 feet long and 225 feet wide and had 127 columns, each 60 feet high and 36 of them richly sculptured. The huge roof was constructed of planks of cedar, and the doors were made of cyprus. The first-century A.D. Roman historian Pliny the Elder wrote that most writers believed the statue within was made of ebony. Pliny also mentioned that the staircase leading to the roof was constructed from a single vine that had been imported from the Aegean island of Cyprus. (Vines reportedly grew to an extraordinarily large size on that island.)

The placing of the roof beams on top of the columns was a feat in itself. Workers hauled the beams up ramps made of sandbags that were piled higher than the columns. As the sand was released from the lower bags, the beams settled permanently into place.

This immense monument to a much-revered goddess took many years to complete. It became known not only for the splendor of its architecture and decorations but also for the richness and beauty of the

20

treasures within. Nations from all over Asia continued to deposit their riches and precious works of art in the temple for as long as the cult of Artemis prevailed.

In A.D. 262, during the reign of the Roman emperor Gallienus, the temple was plundered and burned by invading Goths from northern Europe. It was never restored. A new religion, Christianity, had been gaining strength and had begun to draw followers from the worshipers of Artemis. Eventually, Christianity became the official religion of the Roman Empire.

Since the late 1800s, excavators have been uncovering fragments and artifacts in ancient Ephesos. The remains show that several temples were constructed on the same site. Visitors to Ephesos today can walk along the ancient streets, imagining the grandeur and beauty of this once bustling metropolis.

THE PHAROS OF ALEXANDRIA

In 525 B.C., the Persian king Cambyses attacked and conquered Egypt. Egypt won its independence from Persian control in 404 B.C., but only until 343 B.C., when Egyptian troops were defeated by another Persian king, Artaxerxes III. A decade later, in 332 B.C., the Macedonian king Alexander the Great entered Egypt. The Persian satrap (governor) surrendered to the mighty Alexander without a battle, and Egypt became part of Alexander's empire.

Alexander planned a new city to replace the old Egyptian capital of Memphis. He chose a site at the western end of the Nile Delta and named it Alexandria. He wanted his city built on a mile-and-a-half-wide strip of land between the Mediterranean Sea and Lake Mareotis. Alexander reasoned that the new city's position would give it two harbors, making it a principal port serving the sea trade as well as that of the Nile River.[1] Of the eighteen Alexandrias founded by Alexander, this settlement in Egypt would endure and become a rich center of culture.

Alexander asked the famous architect Deinokrates of Rhodes to design his glorious metropolis. Streets were laid out in an orderly manner, and a splendid boulevard one hundred feet wide and lined with columns ran the length of the city. Huge parks, magnificent palaces, a

---

1. The Egyptians had dug a series of canals to connect Lake Mareotis with the Nile.

THE WORD 'PHAROS'

Constructed of gleaming white marble, the lighthouse at Alexandria stood on the island of Pharos in the city's harbor, hence its name the Pharos of Alexandria. Through the centuries, the word "pharos" has been adopted in different forms as the word for "lighthouse" in several languages. In Latin, a lighthouse is *pharus*; in French, it is *phare*; in Italian and Spanish, it is *faro*; in Portuguese, it is *farol*; and, until recently, pharos was used in English to refer to a lighthouse or beacon.

zoo, a museum, and a library that would become the repository for scholars throughout the ancient world were included in the plans. Egypt's Alexandria was to be a monument to the creator of an empire.

But in 323 B.C., before his dreams could come true, Alexander died unexpectedly in Babylon. Ptolemy Soter, a Macedonian Greek general and Alexander's successor as ruler of Egypt, carried on the scheme initiated by his predecessor. Several years later, when the city was completed, Ptolemy had the remains of the great conqueror placed in a coffin of gold and laid to rest in a mausoleum of great beauty. (The coffin was replaced by one made of glass a century later.)

Around 290 B.C., Ptolemy Soter started planning the construction of a lighthouse to guide ships toward the harbor of Alexandria. He died in 283/2 B.C., before the project was completed. The towering landmark, designed by Sostrates of Knidos, was completed in about 280 B.C. under Ptolemy Soter's son, Ptolemy Philadelphus.

The lighthouse, with its many stories, each smaller than the one below it, soared almost six hundred feet into the sky. The marble blocks were welded together with molten lead instead of cement so the building would withstand the constant pounding of the water. The base was a heavy stone platform upon which was built a massive square building that housed numerous government offices, military barracks, and stables for several hundred horses. The next level contained a broad balcony where

Opposite: On the beach near Alexandria, the remains of an old *pharos*, identical in shape to the famed Pharos of Alexandria, still stands guard.

TALL TALES

Many exaggerated tales were told of the capabilities of the Pharos of Alexandria. It was said that a huge glass or polished metal mirror helped send beams of light far out to sea. It also was said that the Pharos could set enemy ships afire by reflecting the rays of the sun god's flaming chariot. Some people claimed that anyone who looked into the mirror could see as far as Byzantium, in Asia Minor (present-day Istanbul, Turkey). Although these tales may be false, it is certain that this beacon was the most powerful ever created and continued to guide ships into the harbor for hundreds of years.

refreshments were sold to tourists. Another balcony, about three hundred or four hundred feet higher, became the lookout point for sightseers. The final section, rising hundreds of feet above sea level, was cylindrical in shape and contained a beacon chamber at the summit where a fire burned continuously in a great brazier (metal pan). Horses carried fuel up an inclined plane that gradually ascended the lower half of the tower. The fuel was then hoisted to the top through a central shaft by means of a windlass (a drum or cylinder wound with rope and turned with a crank).

As the centuries passed, Alexandria's fame grew throughout the ancient world. Even after the death of Cleopatra VII (a Ptolemy descendant) in 30 B.C., when Egypt became a province of Rome, Alexandria continued to be one of the world's most respected intellectual centers. With the breakup of the Roman Empire in the fourth century A.D. and the subsequent collapse of Rome in the next century, the city lost its prominence. When Egypt fell under Arab control in the seventh century, the capital moved from Alexandria to Cairo. Yet the lighthouse stood as a landmark to the engineering and architectural capabilities of ancient civilizations until sometime around 1375, when an earthquake destroyed it.

From 305 to 304 B.C., the Macedonian command-er Demetrios attacked the island of Rhodes in the Aegean Sea. In spite of Demetrios's hundreds of ships, tens of thousands of men, and huge war machines, the determination and courage of the Rhodians finally forced him to withdraw. As an offering of thanks to the sun god, Helios, the protecting deity of the island, the Rhodians raised a colossal statue in his honor. Tradition says that the stat-

THE COLOSSOS OF RHODES

In the 17th century, European artists were captivated by ancient art and sculpture. Many incorporated representations of past works into their own works of art, as illustrated by this tapestry of the Colossos now hanging in the Louvre Museum in Paris.

ue was made entirely of the bronze obtained from the siege artillery that Demetrios left behind.

Chares of Lindos, a Rhodian sculptor who had helped defend his city, was asked to design and construct what was to become known as the Colossos, the largest bronze statue ever made. He was a former pupil of Lysippos's, the only sculptor whom Alexander the Great had commissioned to fashion his official statues.

Chares cleverly used the captured siege tower as a scaffold. Stone columns were erected as the main supports of the statue, and iron struts extended out of them to support the statue's bronze skin. The large bronze plates were cast and hammered into shape by craftsmen who were skilled at producing the body armor and greaves (leg armor) for Greek warriors. These plates were then riveted together and to a skeleton of iron rods. This was done only after Chares had personally inspected each plate.

The heavy plates were hauled into place following the same principles the Egyptian pyramid builders had used twenty-two centuries earlier. Chares built a mound of earth around the Colossos that grew to a height of one hundred twenty feet. The workers carried the bronze plates into position up a ramp just as the Egyptians had dragged the huge stones onto the tombs of the ancient pharaohs.

After Helios's crown of spiked rays was riveted into place, the mound of earth was shoveled away, the bronze skin polished, and the scaffold removed. A majestic figure measuring sixty feet around the chest, eleven feet around the thighs, and five feet around the ankles now stood at the entrance to the harbor of Rhodes, a monument to the Rhodians' hard-won freedom.

Unfortunately, the Colossos stood for only fifty-six years, when an earthquake brought it crashing down. Through the years, several attempts were made to reerect the statue, but all efforts failed. It lay where it fell for eight hundred years until it was sold as scrap metal.

TIME LINE OF ANCIENT WONDERS

You Need
ruler
pencil
piece of blue construction paper measuring 24 by 18 inches
black felt-tip marker
crayons or paints (tan, green, yellow, white, maroon, orange, and brown)

1. With a ruler and pencil, divide the construction paper lengthwise into nine 2-inch-wide rows.

2. Use the black marker to darken the lines dividing the rows.

3. Across the top row, print or write "Time Line of Ancient Wonders" with the marker.

4. Measure 4 inches from the left side of the construction paper. Draw a vertical line and darken it with the marker.

5. Divide the remaining 20 inches into twenty 1-inch-wide columns. Darken the lines with the marker.

6. In the first column of the second row, write "Ancient Wonder" with the marker.

7. Using the marker and beginning with the line marking the first column, write, in chronological order above each line in the second row, the following dates: 2500, 2275, 2050, 1825, 1600, 1375, 1150, 925, 700, 475, 250, 25, 200, 425, 650, 875, 1100, 1325, 1550, 1775, 2000. (Note: Each block represents a period of 225 years.)

8. Above the block separating the numbers 25 and 200, write "B.C." with an arrow pointing left and "A.D." with an arrow pointing right.

9. In the 4-inch column on the left, write, in chronological order, the name of each wonder and the city where it stood:

Great Pyramid, Giza
Hanging Gardens, Babylon
Statue of Zeus, Olympia
Mausoleum, Halikarnassos
Temple of Artemis, Ephesos
Pharos, Alexandria
Colossos, Rhodes

10. Reread each article and find when the construction of each wonder began. Mark the date in pencil in the appropriate box opposite the wonder's name.

11. Find the date when each wonder was finally destroyed and mark that in the appropriate box. If the wonder still

– illustrated by Annette Cate

Whew, this lightning bolt is hot!

Hurry, let me put it on the chart!

13. stands, put an arrow pointing right in the last box.

12. Using crayons or paints, color in the period of time during which each wonder existed. The color used represents one of the construction materials used:

Pyramid: tan for the limestone
Gardens: green for the trees and plants
Zeus: yellow for the gold
Mausoleum: white for the marble
Artemis: maroon for the vine used to make the stairs

Well, I'll be!

Pharos: orange for the flame
Colossos: brown for the bronze

13. You might want to add a symbol that shows the destruction of the wonder. A zigzag would mean a natural disaster, such as an earthquake; a bow and arrow would mean human intervention, such as war.

14. Compare the lengths of time the wonders stood and how they met their ends.

MAKE A LEGEND

lines nice and straight!

You might want to add a legend to explain the colors used to represent each wonder and the symbols used to represent the means of destruction.

Always measure carefully!

LEGEND

| NAME OF WONDER | COLOR AND SYMBOL | EXPLANATION OF COLOR AND SYMBOL |

make 3 columns!

Label your columns!

I always thought limestone should be lime-colored!

LEGEND

GREAT PYRAMID GIZA		COLOR OF LIMESTONE
HANGING GARDENS BABYLON		
STATUE OF ZEUS		

You Need
ruler
pencil
piece of blue construction paper measuring 6 by 4 1/2 inches
black felt-tip marker
crayons

Blue

1. With the ruler and pencil, divide the construction paper into 1/2-inch-wide horizontal rows. Darken the lines with the marker.

2. Across the top, write "Legend" with the marker.

3. Divide the remaining rows into three 2-inch-wide vertical columns.

4. On the second row, write "Name of Wonder," "Color and Symbol," and "Explanation of Color and Symbol" in marker over columns 1, 2, and 3, respectively.

5. Fill in the names of the seven wonders in the first column.

6. Color in the middle column to correspond to the color used to represent each wonder. Then add the symbols you used on the time line.

7. In the third column, add the reason for the color used and what the symbol represents.

8. Affix the legend to the back of the time line or an unused area on the front.

Affix means to stick on!

LEGEND

CROSSWORD PUZZLE

ACROSS

2. He designed the Colossos of Rhodes
5. What a mausoleum is
7. Temple scenes often show these mythical people fighting with Centaurs
10. Great river in Egypt
11. They plundered and burned the temple at Ephesos
15. Greek sculptors used this color to represent flesh
16. Spanish word for lighthouses
17. First-century B.C. Greek historian
18. One of the colors Greek sculptors used for draperies
21. Olympia is located on this Greek peninsula
23. Egyptian pyramid builders worked in _____-month shifts
25. The opposite of B.C.
26. Used to carry fuel for the Pharos
28. The mightiest of Greek gods
30. Where Lydia and Ephesos were
31. Used to construct Colossos of Rhodes
32. Number of wonders that were tombs
33. Architect who designed Alexandria
35. Alexandria had one of these
36. Greek city-state where Olympia is located
37. Pyramids housed their remains
38. Where Mausolos ruled

DOWN

1. Zeus at Olympia held a statue of her
3. The patron god of Rhodes
4. Greek sculptor who worked on Mausolos's tomb
6. City of Babylon had fifty-five miles of these
7. The blocks used to build pyramids were made of this
8. Famed Greek writer
9. Latin word for pharos
12. These formed the base of the Hanging Gardens
13. King of Babylon
14. The Mausoleum's columns were made of this material
19. It destroyed Pharos
20. Alexander the Great's coffin was made of this
21. Greek traveler and geographer
22. He designed the Pharos
24. Where pyramids are
27. Alexander's successor as ruler of Egypt
29. Egypt became one of its provinces in 30 B.C.
34. Used to prevent the ivory in Zeus's statue from cracking

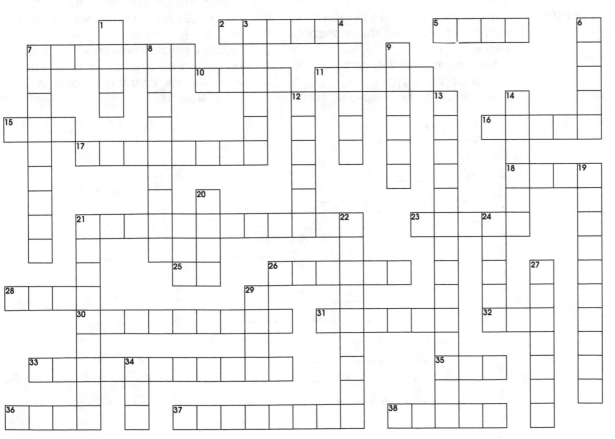

Answers to these puzzles can be found in this chapter and on page 144.

PHILON'S SITES AND SIGHTS

Can you match the ancient site with the sight(s) located there?

1. Five temples were erected to Artemis at this site. _____

2. Nebuchadrezzar II built gardens for his queen, who felt that this city was too hot. _____

3. The people here built a statue of Helios in thanks for a military victory. _____

4. A lighthouse welcomed ships into this city's harbor. _____

5. Artemisia's monument to her husband here became her mausoleum also. _____

6. Pheidias sculpted the statue of Zeus here. _____

7. Khufu built his pyramid here. _____

a. Olympia
b. Alexandria
c. Giza
d. Ephesos
e. Rhodes
f. Babylon
g. Halikarnassos

A COMMON NEIGHBOR

Use the clues to fill in the blanks. The letters in the boxes will spell the name of a neighbor common to every country that housed an ancient wonder.

1. This king gave his name to a monument built to house his remains.

2. The island of Rhodes is located here. (two words)

3. The roof of Artemis's temple was made of this wood.

4. Many of Artemis's worshipers left to follow this religion.

5. What the Pharos at Alexandria really was.

6. The sculptor Pheidias lived in this country.

7. The wood of Khufu's boat was so strong that it resisted these animals. (two words)

8. Alexander gave this name to his new capital of Egypt.

9. Her tribute to her husband's memory became a wonder of the world.

10. Istanbul is the present name of ancient Byzantium. What other name did this city once have?

11. The Greeks instituted these games to pay special tribute to Zeus. (two words)

12. This king gave the columns for Artemis's fourth temple at Ephesos. What was the name of his country?

13. These were Nebuchadrezzar's attempt at air conditioning.

14. Two Greek sculptors who went to work for Artemisia.

15. Zeus's statue was made of this.

16. Two famed sculptors: One was from Rhodes, and the other was from Greece.

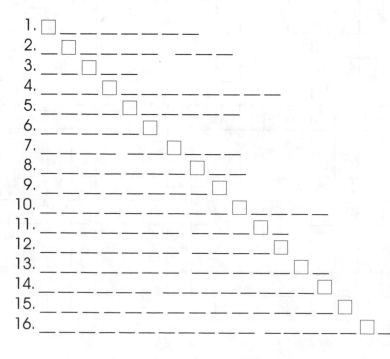

COMPANION 1

Topics for Comparison

1. Compare and contrast seven modern wonders with the ancient wonders. Modern wonders may include the Crystal Palace in London (1851), the Statue of Liberty in New York City (1886), the Eiffel Tower in Paris (1889), the Trans Siberian Railroad in Russia (1905), the Panama Canal (1914), the Empire State Building in New York City (1931), and the Golden Gate Bridge in San Francisco (1937).

2. Through the centuries, many of the materials used to build the wonders were recycled and used in the construction of other structures. Compare this practice with the recycling of buildings going on throughout the United States today.

3. Both the Mausoleum at Halikarnassos and the Taj Mahal in India were built to honor dead spouses. Compare and contrast the circumstances under which they were built.

4. Erecting monuments to honor the dead is a time-honored practice. The Great Pyramid and the Mausoleum are just two of many such monuments. Compare the latter with other structures built to house the bodies of honored leaders (for example, Grant's Tomb in Riverside Park, New York City, and the Invalides in Paris).

5. It would be very difficult for a ruler today to build a hanging garden, pyramid, or mausoleum. Why? Compare and contrast the reasons such constructions were possible in ancient times but are not possible in the present.

6. The main purpose of the Pharos of Alexandria was to act as a lighthouse, but it also attracted many tourists. List some modern structures that have had a similar history, then compare and contrast the examples you give.

7. The Colossos of Rhodes was built as a monument to a victory. Compare this monument with those built in modern times to celebrate a victory. Two examples are the Iwo Jima monument and the Arc de Triomphe in Paris.

8. The wonders of the world are just larger and more magnificent than similar, smaller structures. Countless small mausoleums have been built. Ports and shoals everywhere have lighthouses to guide incoming and passing vessels. Many new shopping malls and business complexes have indoor hanging gardens and mock waterfalls. Massive religious buildings, such as the Church of St. John the Divine in New York City and the National Cathedral in Washington, D.C., are still in the process of being built. Take a look around your neighborhood, city, and/or state and find a monument to compare and contrast with one of the ancient wonders.

Suggestions for Writing Assignments

1. What criteria determine what is a wonder and what is not?

2. What criteria would you establish to determine whether a wonder should be classified as such?

3. Do you agree with the choice of modern wonders? Would you delete any? Why? Would you add any? Why?

4. Was each civilization at its peak when the wonder was constructed? What does this tell you about the civilization?

5. What does the type of construction and the reason for the construction tell you about the people who built a wonder? Were they prosperous? Was their nation at peace? How did the climate relate to such a lengthy undertaking?

6. Architectural wonders are sources of national pride. How do the ancient and modern wonders reflect this?

Further Activities

1. Reread the description of each ancient wonder. Then try to reconstruct one either as a drawing or a three-dimensional figure. (This may be done as a class project. Divide the class into groups and allow each group to choose a wonder to replicate.)

2. The ancients provided us with the dimensions of certain parts of the Colossos. Take a tape measure and find an object in your area that measures five feet in diameter (the measurement given for each of the Colossos's ankles). Try experimenting with the other measurements as well.

3. Create your own wonder. Determine the criteria that would make your creation qualify as a wonder. Specify the purpose of your creation. Draw up the dimensions. Tell where it would be located and why you would choose that particular area. Give the probability of its being used.

4. Find out what the seven natural wonders of the world are and the criteria for their being named natural wonders.

5. Research the story of Pelops and Oenomaos and the origin of the Olympic Games.

6. Research the tale of the Centaurs and the Lapiths.

Topics for Debate

1. The time and expense required to build a wonder would be put to better use if spent on humanitarian purposes.

2. Only during times of prosperity can a people create a structure or work of art worthy of being recognized as a wonder.

"Life is short, art is long."

Hippocrates (c. 460–c. 377 B.C.), Greek physician

THE CLASSICAL TEMPLE

CHAPTER 2

THE ACROPOLIS

Rising approximately two hundred sixty feet above modern Athens and measuring one thousand feet long and four hundred feet at its widest part, this enormous rock ledge served as a fortress for the first Athenians. It was known as an acropolis, a combination of the Greek words *akros* (highest) and *polis*[1] (city). Although this term originally referred to the citadel or fortress of any city, as Athens assumed the role of a world power, its magnificent rock ledge became the Acropolis of the ancient world.

The early kings, such as Kekrops and Erichthonios, built their palaces on the Acropolis. However, as Athens grew in size and importance, the ledge became an area sacred to the city's patron deities and to legendary Athenian heroes. Around the seventh century B.C., all private dwellings were relocated at the base of the Acropolis.

When the Persians entered Athens in 480 B.C., they destroyed and burned the Acropolis. After the Greeks had time to regroup, they routed the Persian forces first at Salamis in September of 480 B.C. and then at Plataiai in 479 B.C.

Thirty years later, the master Athenian statesman and general Pericles commissioned the architects Iktinos and Kallikrates and the famed sculptor Pheidias to design a religious center on the Acropolis as an everlasting memorial to Greece's hard-won victory over Persia. The result of their combined efforts, which included the construction of the Parthenon, the Propylaia, and the Erechtheion, made the Acropolis the world-famous monument of the classical period of architecture.

The Acropolis, with the majestic remains of the Parthenon, stands above present-day Athens.

---

1. The English words "metropolis," "police," "cosmopolitan," and "politics" are all derived from the Greek *polis*.

THE PARTHENON

The Parthenon, the magnificent fifth-century B.C. temple built by the Athenians for their patron goddess Athena,[1] was one of the finest temples ever built. Its unequaled beauty and serene simplicity summarize ancient Greece's legacy to the Western world.

The grillwork of the doors allowed the sun to cast its light on the enormous forty-two-foot statue of Athena standing at the western end of the *naos*.[2] This exquisitely carved work of the Greek sculptor Pheidias represented the goddess of wisdom fully armed and holding a statue of Nike, the winged goddess of victory, in her right hand. The drapery, armor, and accessories of the wooden statue were formed of detachable gold plates. The face, hands, and feet were of ivory, and the eyes were of precious stones.

To add to the grandeur, the interior of the naos was divided into three aisles by two rows of two-tiered columns (one row of columns set above another). The statue was located in the central spot, at the end of the middle aisle and in front of another row of tiered columns.

---

1. The Parthenon derived its name from the goddess Athena, who was known as Athena Parthenos, or Athena "the maiden goddess."

2. The Greek term *naos* also is used to refer to the chamber where the image of the deity stood.

THE PROPYLAIA

This massive marble structure, which incorporated into its design the entrance to the Acropolis, was begun under Pericles in approximately 438 B.C. Unfortunately, the Peloponnesian War (the great war between the Greek city-states of Athens and Sparta) intervened, and all work was halted in 431 B.C. The basic plan included five gates, with the largest in the middle. To the east and west of these gates were porticoes (porches). The completed north wing housed a small hall and a large chamber. The south wing was to be identical to the north but was never completed.

Exterior Doric columns still decorate the façade of the Propylaia, the entrance to the Acropolis.

THE ERECHTHEION

Named in honor of Erichthonios, one of the first kings of Athens, this temple was originally the sanctuary of the divine protectors of Athens—Athena, the goddess of wisdom, and Poseidon, the god of the sea. The ancient authors wrote that the rock ledge on the north side still bore the marks made by Poseidon's trident during his contest with Athena to determine who would be Athens's patron. There, too, the ancients built a chamber to enclose a fountain sacred to Poseidon. On the south side was a corresponding chamber housing Athena's gift to Athens, the sacred olive tree. During the wars with Persia, the tree was burned, but, miraculously, it immediately put forth a new shoot.

The most famous section of the building was the porch of the maidens on the south side. Instead of columns to support the roof, pillars were sculptured in the shape of draped women, with the capitals (top part of the pillar) above their heads resembling baskets. As such, they were reminiscent of the young women who carried baskets on their heads in the solemn procession during Athena's Great Panathenaic Festival.

These karyatides, as pillars in the shape of maidens were called, presented to the observer a sense of strength and firmness. Through careful and deliberate placement of the hair, the architects strengthened their necks, which was necessary for the burden these maidens carried. The sculptors also crafted the maidens so that they seemed to place their weight on one leg, giving them the appearance of elasticity and power.

The Erechtheion, with its porch of karyatides, was the most elegant building on the Acropolis.

THE RAVAGES OF TIME

Archaeologists and historians treasure the well-preserved description of the Acropolis written by the second-century A.D. Greek traveler and geographer Pausanias because, only two hundred years later, the Roman emperor Theodosius ordered his soldiers to destroy pagan monuments throughout the empire. A few buildings were spared and used for other purposes. The Parthenon was one. It later became a Christian church.

When the Turks conquered Greece in the late fourteenth century, they seized the Acropolis and added minarets to the Parthenon to make it into a mosque. They also stored gunpowder in the temple. In 1687, when the Turks were at war with the Venetians, a cannon shot pierced the Parthenon's roof and ignited the gunpowder. The damage was devastating and irreparable. The magnificent structures that had survived the centuries were in ruins. No attempt at restoration was made. Rather, the marble pieces were used in other structures.

In recent years, the Greek government has enacted several laws aimed at controlling the damage being done to the Acropolis because of pollution, acid rain, and faulty restoration efforts. Tourists are no longer allowed to enter the temples. Vehicular traffic is banned from the road leading up to the Acropolis, and residents in buildings adjacent to the Acropolis are restricted as to the type of heating fuel they may use.

In 1985, Greece entered into an agreement with the European Economic Community to begin restoring the Acropolis. The project is not expected to be completed until after the year 2000. The archaeologists, historians, engineers, and scientists involved in this project hope to correct mistakes made by past restorers, stabilize the structures that still exist, and restore hundreds of walls and columns that have fallen.

THE GREEK TEMPLE

The term "temple" originally referred to areas of sacred land, natural caves, or hollow trees. Sometimes a sacred stone or an altar was placed in a selected area to symbolize a divine presence and a place of sacrifice. Gradually, architects began designing structures to enclose these sacred areas. Because the ancients considered these sites the earthly homes of their deities and not an area for people to gather, a large interior was unnecessary. The Greeks called their temple *naos,* which means "dwelling place." Because religious ceremonies and sacrifices were held in the open spaces and on the altars outside the temple, it was opened only on special occasions, if at all.

The first temple structure consisted of a small boxlike building. Frequently, a long, narrow opening in the roof allowed light to enter. Later, columns were placed in front between projecting side walls. As the decades passed, more columns were added to the front and to the back and sides.

The Greeks had a superb sense of beauty and proportion, which they used to modify, supplement, and alter their architectural styles. The simple tree-trunk columns of the early wooden structures gave way to cut and fashioned wooden columns. Bricks were used to build porticoes. To separate the bricks from the damp ground, a stone wall about two feet high was incorporated into the temple design. For strength, the crude bricks, made of gravel, pounded pottery, and clay mixed with chopped straw, were usually allowed to dry for several years before being used. Gradually, stone or marble replaced wood and bricks, radically changing the character of the temple.

A substructure, called the stereobate, provided added strength and protection for the temple. This below-ground foundation was usually rectangular in shape. Above it was the stylobate, or base, which formed the steps of the temple and was composed of more carefully dressed (cut and smoothed) rows of blocks. The usual number of steps was three, and the height of each step was determined by the height of the stylobate. The steps of the great temples such as the Parthenon were so high that smaller, intermediate steps were added at convenient places to allow for easier entrance.

The stone blocks were quarried by slaves and then sent down mountainside chutes into wagons pulled by thirty to forty oxen. At the building site, state-hired workers did the actual construction work using derricks, wooden scaffolding, and lathes.

On the stylobate was a rectangular cell-like structure. Much more massive and detailed than its earlier counterpart, it served the same purpose—to provide an earthly home for a god. The windowless walls were of solid stone or marble. Extra care was taken so that each block, especially those of marble, fit closely to the next. The blocks were cut and then rubbed to obtain the smoothest possible surface.

Once a block was set in place, it was moved backward and forward until the slow grinding of the stone bonded block to block and created a perfect fit. Hence, there was no need to use cement or mortar. To further strengthen the walls, the ancient Greeks used bronze or iron clamps and dowels to fasten each block in place. In the Parthenon, every block was clamped to its horizontally adjacent block and fixed with dowels (metal plugs) to its vertically adjacent block.

Although the Greeks modified and corrected their designs in numerous ways as they strove to create a perfect structure, they never added anything unnecessary. Even ornamentation served a purpose. For example, the simple decoration on the capitals allowed the spectator's eye to pass smoothly from the columns to the entablature (upper level). So magnificent was the Greek temple that it still remains an unsurpassed tribute to the glory of Greece.

INSIDE THE GREEK TEMPLE

Temples were usually built facing east. Their massive doors, which opened out, were often gold plated and covered with gold and ivory relief designs. The interiors of these sacred buildings varied in design and detail according to the size and grandeur of the temple.

Often the ceilings were coffered, or composed of deeply recessed marble or ornamental stone panels. Columns also served to support the decoratively painted wooden roof timbers above the *naos,* the chamber housing the image of the deity.

The floor was usually formed of large slabs of stone or marble. In the Parthenon, as in most temples, the central portion of the naos's floor was slightly sunken.

Many temples had a special chamber called the *opisthodomos* where worshipers' offerings were placed. Also known as the treasury, this area in the most venerated temples became so filled with offerings that small treasure houses had to be built nearby to accommodate the many gifts of the faithful.

Within each temple, one section was designated as the god's special home. Located directly behind the naos and facing west, this area was usually open only to priests and priestesses. Entrance into it was through the opisthodomos. In smaller temples, elaborate bronze screens or grilles separated this sacred area from the more open area of the temple.

THE THREE ORDERS

The dominant feature of every fifth-century B.C. temple was its columns. Rectangular temples were classed according to the arrangement of the columns and the number of columns in front. Thus, the Parthenon is peripteral octastyle. Peripteral, from the Greek words *peri* (around) and *pteron* (wing), means that it has columns along both sides and the ends. Octastyle, from the Greek word *octo* (eight), means that it has eight columns in front.

As the temples increased in size, so did the columns. Single drums or columns became impractical and impossible. Instead, drums were cut horizontally into sections to be reassembled at the site. To facilitate reassembly, the masons left small blocks of marble projecting from each piece of the drum. Ropes were looped around these projections. At the building site, the workmen used these ropes to help them set each section in place and then to revolve the drum until each section fit perfectly into the one below it.

Three basic architectural orders (styles of columns) developed: Doric, Ionic, and Corinthian.

DORIC

The simplest of the three, the Doric column symbolized strength and solidarity. It had no base but stood directly on the stylobate. Its circular shaft was fluted (usually with twenty vertical ridges). Atop each column rested a capital consisting of three sections: (1) the annulets, or horizontal flat moldings, (2) the echinus,[1] or curved circular disk, and (3) the abacus, or square unmolded slab of stone. Doric capitals were never decorated. The height of a Doric column (including the capi-

---

1. In defining the sections of the ancient temple, we have opted to used the Latin forms for two reasons: This chapter includes articles about Greek and Roman temples, and the spelling most commonly found in books on architecture is the Latin form of the Greek term.

tal) was four to six and a half times the diameter of the column's base (page 42).

IONIC

The Ionic column was more graceful and refined. Originating in the eastern Greek towns of Asia Minor (present-day Turkey), this style was inspired by the art of the Orient. Taller and more slender than the Doric column, the Ionic stood on a molded base. Its height was nine times the lower diameter of its column. The flutes of the Ionic style were deeper and narrower.

The distinguishing characteristic was the column's capital, which was separated from the main shaft by a molding, above which was a band carved with a design of palm leaves or water lilies. The capital itself consisted of a pair of volutes, or spiral scrolls, on the front and rear of the column. These spirals were connected by an echinus. The side molding was a simple, cushion-shaped band. The front and rear moldings were carved with an egg-and-dart design (top right).

CORINTHIAN

The third order, the Corinthian, was easily recognized by its capital. The Greeks rarely used this order, perhaps because they felt that its ornamentation detracted from the sim-

THE ANCIENT BLOCK MOVERS

The ancients left few written accounts of their building methods. However, several building contracts do exist. These contracts list the materials needed, the equipment used, and the costs involved in transporting the stone blocks from the quarry to the building site. Still, it is the stone block itself that provides the best account of building methods.

Careful and detailed study of the remains at each site has helped historians and architects reconstruct the building methods used. Each block's grooves, indentations, lumps, and holes are studied separately and then in relation to those on other blocks surrounding it. The findings are compared with past findings and with descriptions of hoisting machines found in ancient works, especially *The Ten Books of Architecture* by the first-century B.C. Roman writer and architect Vitruvius.

Using levers, pulleys, and pulley blocks, workers raised the blocks from the ground to their final resting place on the building. Workers at ground level and on scaffolding helped complete the task. Clamps (metal bars) and dowels (metal plugs) were used instead of cement or mortar to fasten the blocks together. The grooves, slots, and holes made to hold the clamps and dowels are still recognizable today.

After workers placed a stone properly, they cleaned the joint with bicarbonate of soda before rinsing it with clean water. A supervisor inspected every joint to determine whether it was tight enough. If it was, the workers poured molten lead around the clamps and dowels until every crack was filled. This final step ensured secure and immovable stones.

plicity they believed a temple required.

According to a Greek legend, the Corinthian capital's form originated in the city of Corinth, in central Greece. A young girl had died, and her nurse had put a basket filled with all the girl's favorite belongings on her grave. To keep everything in place, the nurse had placed a tile over the basket. The following spring, the leaves of a nearby acanthus plant completely surrounded the basket. When the famed Greek sculptor Kallimachos passed the spot, the beauty of this basket surrounded by acanthus leaves so entranced him that he created a new capital and named it Corinthian.

Whatever the origin, the Corinthian capital does resemble a basket or inverted bell, the lower part of which is surrounded by two rows of eight acanthus leaves. From between the leaves of the upper row rise other elongated leaves and volutes, which support the abacus. Each side of the molded abacus curves outward to a point at the edges.

The remaining columns of the 2nd-century B.C. temple of Olympian Zeus at Athens near the Acropolis are excellent examples of the Corinthian order of architecture.

The section above the columns was known as the entablature. It was composed of three main divisions: the architrave, the frieze, and the cornice. The treatment of these sections corresponded to the order of the columns used. Thus, the Doric entablature was simpler than the Ionic and Corinthian entablatures.

The architrave, or principal beam, was composed of long blocks of stone, each bridging two columns and extending halfway across the capitals of the two columns. The upper part of the architrave formed a flat molding with a narrow band from which extended six *guttae,* or small conical drops. So symmetrical and methodical were the Greek architects that each group of guttae was positioned below a projecting triglyph (a section of the frieze).

The frieze was composed of alternating triglyphs (three vertical stone channels) and metopes. By custom and design, triglyphs were centered over each column and over the space between the columns. Metopes, the square spaces between the triglyphs, were usually decorated with groups of finely sculptured figures. Doric entablatures had metopes and triglyphs; Ionic and Corinthian entablatures had a continuous sculptured frieze.

Perhaps the most famous metopes are those known as the Elgin Marbles. In the early 1800s, Lord Elgin of England was assigned as an envoy to Constantinople (present-day Istanbul, Turkey). A lover of antiquities, Lord Elgin feared that the animosity between the Greeks and the Turks, who controlled Greece at that time, might cause irreparable harm to the metopes adorning the Parthenon. Therefore, he requested the Turks' permission to measure and sketch the ancient monuments for posterity. After his request was granted, Lord Elgin proceeded to send various artifacts, including the Parthenon's metopes, to London, where they are now housed in the British Museum.[1]

The cornice supported the roof of the temple. It also sheltered the frieze and the architrave because it jutted out beyond them. Doric architecture dictat-ed that small, flat, square blocks (mutules) or small, projecting, rectangular blocks (dentils) be placed on the underside of the slightly sloping cornice. Ionic and Corinthian temples had a continuous row of dentils above the frieze.

The entablature supported both the roof and the pediment, the triangular space above either end of a Greek temple. Usually, this space was filled with sculptured reliefs depicting a myth involving the temple's deity.

Although traces of bright colors have been found on sculptures from pediments, friezes, and metopes, color usually was restricted to the detailed reliefs. Archaeologists believe that this was done to accent the designs of areas farthest away. Also, because the sun reflected the brilliance of the marble walls and columns, the addition of color softened the effect of the temple and enhanced the beauty of the sculp-tured details. Red was used for the architrave and the lower molding of the cornice; blue was used for the triglyphs and mutules. The guttae often were yellow or gilt with gold, and the metopes were white. If the metopes were sculptured, the back-ground was painted red or blue.

The roof was made of strong rafters covered with baked clay tiles or slabs of white marble closely joined to prevent leaks. At the end of each row of jointed tiles was an *antefixa*, an ornament usually sculptured to resemble a lotus flower or an acanthus leaf. Sculptured lions' heads often were placed at intervals along the eaves. These acted as spouts for rainwater, which then fell into a gutter around the stylobate and was carried in pipes or open channels to tanks near the temple.

---

1. Lord Elgin's treasures were shipped to England over a period of ten years, from 1802 to 1812. The British Crown bought the entire collection in 1816. Today the question of who owns the Elgin Marbles is a matter of great dispute. Greece would like to see them returned to the country of their origin. England feels that because it ensured their safekeeping, it should retain possession.

ROME'S ARCHITECTURAL LEGACY

As the Roman world grew in size and power, Rome found its buildings too small to accommodate the daily business of its inhabitants and the hordes of people flocking to the capital city. Roman architects and engineers soon realized the limitations of the Greek temple design that they had borrowed.

With its simple column and architrave (the flat stone blocks resting on the columns), the Greek temple did not lend itself to much adaptation. Furthermore, the comparatively small, enclosed areas within the Greek temple did not lend themselves to public use. The Romans needed a design that would allow them to span large, open areas and that would, in turn, create buildings with immense interiors.

The arch, formed by a series of wedge-like stones or bricks supporting each other and bound firmly together by mutual pressure, constitutes the main distinction between Greek and Roman architecture. The Romans used the vault and the dome in combination with the arch. Although not the originators of these designs, the Romans took the initiative in adopting, modifying, and expanding all three.

GREEK VERSUS ROMAN

The Greeks were a very religious people and centered their architectural endeavors on their temples. These structures, though relatively small, were architectural masterpieces. The Romans concentrated their efforts on buildings that served the worldly needs of the peoples and nations they governed, such as aqueducts, baths, circuses, law courts, and

MAGRIPPA·L·F·COS·TERTIVM·FECIT

theaters. Thus, the architecture of these ancient civilizations reflected their lifestyles and philosophies.

The qualities essential to all Greek temples were simplicity, unity of form, and symmetry. The Greek temple was a self-contained unit, standing alone (often on a hill), apart from business and residential areas. Although the Roman temple resembled the Greek temple, the Romans built their temples in populated areas. As was characteristic of this energetic and powerful race, the plans of their buildings conveyed vastness, magnificence, and strength.

Begun in 27 B.C. by the Roman statesman Agrippa, the Pantheon was completed by the emperor Hadrian sometime between A.D. 118 and 128. The Corinthian columns along its façade supported a triangular pediment. The main body of the temple was a circular drum strengthened with enormous brick arches and covered by a magnificent dome.

Instead of using the Greek temple's low stylobate, the Romans placed their temple floor on a raised platform with a stairway across the front. This added to the grandeur, as it attracted and raised the onlooker's eye to the temple's entrance.

The Greeks built their temples facing east, so that the rising sun would illuminate the deity's statue positioned opposite the entrance door. The Romans concerned themselves primarily with easy access and had their temples face the forum, or marketplace.

One of the most admirable features of the Greek temple was its construction out of huge, rectangular stone or marble blocks. The Romans revolutionized the art of building when they introduced concrete made of lime, pozzolana (a volcanic rock), and broken fragments of stone. No longer were large slabs of granite needed. To build very thick walls, the Romans made the sides, or facings, of stone and brick and fashioned the core (the middle section) of fragments of these materials. Concrete was usually used for the foundations and sometimes as a facing for walls.

The interior of the Roman temple (*naos* in Greek and *cella* in Latin) was usually wider and larger than its Greek counterpart. Some Roman temples even had windows. Both nations used coffered ceilings of stone or marble, but the Greeks tended to use wooden timbers for the ceiling above the naos. Both also used their temples to store state treasures and often the wealth of private citizens.

Perhaps the most often imitated and striking features of the ancients' temples were the columns, the entablature, and the pediment. The columns and the flat beam above them, known as post-and-lintel architecture, were the hallmark of Greek architecture. The Romans varied this style with their addition of the curved arch. Greek columns were usually fluted—that is, marked with vertical ridges. The Romans often left their columns unfluted, especially when they were of veined marble or granite.

The Greeks used three orders of architecture (types of columns): Doric, Ionic, and Corinthian. The Romans added the Tuscan and Composite orders.

The favorite and most widely used Greek order was Doric. The Romans rarely used this style because of its severe simplicity. When they did, they modified it in several ways—for example, by adding a base for each column or using unfluted columns or moldings above the abacus.

The Romans sometimes used the Tuscan order, which was a much simpler form of the Greek Doric. It had a base, an unfluted column, a simple capital, and a plain entablature.

Although the Greeks rarely used the Corinthian order because of its ornate capital, the Romans easily adapted its fluted column to accent their larger temples. Whereas the acanthus leaves of the Greek Corinthian capital were of the prickly type and pointed, the Roman capital featured blunt-ended acanthus leaves or olive leaves. Later the Romans introduced brackets, known as modillions, along the cornice.

The Romans had a fifth order of columns, known as the Composite. More ornate than the Corinthian, the Composite had capitals that were a combination of Ionic spirals and Corinthian acanthus leaves.

An architectural feature commonly used by the Romans but not the Greeks was the pilaster. This feature was actually a half column because one side of the pilaster was attached to and formed part of a wall.

The Greek temple was a public expression of the Greeks' love of beauty. In contrast, the Roman temple clearly expressed the Romans' love of power.

GREEK REVIVAL IN THE UNITED STATES

The centuries between the fall of Rome (A.D. 410) and the late Middle Ages (thirteenth century A.D.) witnessed the destruction, complete alteration, or abandonment of many Greek and Roman architectural masterpieces. The Renaissance, the great movement of intellectual rebirth that spread throughout Europe during the fourteenth, fifteenth, and sixteenth centuries, saw a renewed faith in the creative abilities of every human being. When the artists and scholars of this period sought models, they turned to the

The 1st-century B.C. temple built by the Romans in Nîmes, France, served as the model for the state capitol building in Richmond, Virginia.

ancients who had once ruled the Roman world. They read and followed the works of Vitruvius, a first-century B.C. Roman architect. They also studied the Roman ruins that remained or had been converted into churches.

Not until the eighteenth century and the beginning of systematic excavations was the Greek style of architecture understood and appreciated. The ruins of ancient buildings and the many finds that were unearthed so inspired Western architects that a new style of building design developed. This style conformed to the rules of the ancient Greek and Roman architects.

In post-Revolutionary America, the people of the United States found it easy to identify with the culture of ancient Greece and Rome. Thomas Jefferson, the third president of the United States (1801–1809), was a great proponent of the classical style. He designed the state capitol in Richmond, Virginia (built from 1789 to 1798), based on a Roman temple that still stands in Nîmes, France. Other leading architects, such as Benjamin Latrobe and Charles Bulfinch, also designed and promoted the classical style. As a result, many of our customhouses, state capitols, banks, and public buildings reflected the nation's newfound freedom from England and a desire also to be free of England's architectural style.

Although the noble simplicity of the Greek temples inspired the new architects, the size and grandeur of the Roman buildings impressed them even more. Sometimes they built exact replicas of these structures. At other times, they used a particular ancient building as a model. In most instances, the architects combined elements from both the Greek and Roman styles.

American architects were not content with using Greek and Roman structures as models for public buildings. They also incorporated these elements into the designs of their homes. This style was called Greek Revival and was very popular from 1815 to 1860. It was characterized by the use of any of the orders of column architecture, whether they be used on porticoes or on either side of the front entrance. The baseless Greek Doric column was the most commonly used architectural order. However, pilasters were frequently placed on either side of the front door and Ionic pilasters at the corners.

Greek Revival architects favored moderately pitched gable roofs. Sometimes they placed the gable end (the temple pediment) above the front door. At other times, the front door was placed in the middle of the lengthwise side of the structure, with the gables at either end. The doors and windows of these buildings were of the post-and-lintel design—that is, they had a flat top of wood, stone, or marble that resembled the architrave above the temple columns.

The city of Nashville, Tennessee, constructed a temporary replica of the Parthenon to house the international art exhibition for the 1897 Centennial Exposition. In the 1920s, the city's park board, faced with a decaying and unsightly structure, authorized a complete reconstruction using permanent materials.

2

OPTICAL ILLUSIONS

Perhaps the most fascinating characteristic of Greek temple design is its perfect symmetry. The Greeks understood how light plays tricks on the eye. To help you understand this part of Greek design, try the following two experiments.

You Need
piece of Styrofoam measuring 24 by 20 by 2 inches
ruler
pencil
18 empty cardboard tubes (toilet paper rolls work best)
dinner knife or screwdriver
piece of flat cardboard measuring 21 by 17 inches
rags or pieces of cloth (scrap paper can be used if no cloth is available)
scissors
Scotch tape

make sure you use up all the toilet paper first!

1. Make a series of dots 2 inches in from each side of the Styrofoam. Connect the dots.
2. Using one corner of the rectangle as your base, place dots 4 inches apart on the lines.
3. Take one of the empty cardboard tubes and place it over a dot. (Keep the dot exactly in the middle of the tube opening.) Trace a circle around the bottom of the tube. Do the same for every dot.
4. With the dinner knife or screwdriver, carefully press down the Styrofoam along the circles you have made.
5. Place one cardboard tube on each circle. Make sure each tube is secure and can stand by itself.
6. Place the piece of flat cardboard on top of the tubes.
7. Set your "temple" on a table.

– illustrated by Annette Cate

I'm making these dots nice and easy to see!
Always be extra careful!
Give your temple a roof!
the tubes should fit nice and tight!
trace around the tubes!
Wow! Now it's all set for my tiny worshipers to move in!

EXPERIMENT 1

Now you are ready to challenge your eyes. Look at your "temple." Do not stand too close. Remember, the Greek temple stood alone, away from the marketplace and bustling crowds. Does the middle portion of any of the columns appear smaller than the top or bottom of the column?

The Greeks knew that the middle portion of a straight column appears thinner because light from behind the column "eats away" at it. To overcome this optical illusion, the Greeks used entasis — a gentle swelling of the column at the center and a slight tapering toward the top.

To create a bit of a bulge in the middle of your columns, stuff each cardboard tube with rags or scrap paper. Put extra stuffing in as you approach the middle of the tube. Make two 1-inch cuts on either side of the top of each tube. Slightly overlap the cut sides of the tube and seal them with Scotch tape. Replace the flat cardboard piece.

Place the "temple" on the table. Look at the temple from all angles. Do you see how entasis tricks the eye into believing the columns are evenly proportioned from top to bottom?

EXPERIMENT 2

Do the corner columns seem a little thinner than the middle columns? They should, because this is another optical illusion the Greeks had to overcome. Corner columns appear thinner because the background behind them is always brighter than that behind the other columns.

Stuff the corner columns with more rags or paper to make them slightly thicker than the other columns. Remember to keep the bulge in the middle. Now look at your "temple." The optical illusion of thinner corner columns should have disappeared.

Note: Another optical illusion that the Greeks attempted to correct was the apparent "sinking" in the middle of a long horizontal line. This "sinking" detracted from the temple's strong façade, so the Greeks invented ways to fool the eye. They made the steps, the floor of the stylobate, and the lines of the entablature curve very slightly in the middle. (The rise of the curve depended on the size of the temple.)

On Assignment: Next time you see a Greek Revival building, look carefully at the columns. Did the architect use entasis? How did he or she treat the corner columns?

normal column | entasis column

You have to look very carefully to see the difference!

To make Entasis

Stuff the tube with rags or scrap paper!

make one-inch cuts at the top of the tube!

PUZZLE PAGES 2

A JUMBLED FORTRESS

Use the clues listed below to find the twenty-one words hidden in the puzzle. The answers can be found in the articles on the Acropolis, pages 34–39, and on page 146.

Athens's fortress
The patron goddess of Athens
Two Greek city-states
Two structures on the Acropolis
Two kings of Athens
Two Greek architects
Columns in the shape of maidens
The Turks made the Acropolis into this
The temple chamber where the deity's statue stood
The goddess of victory
The war between Athens and Sparta
An Athenian statesman
Enemies of Athens
A Greek sculptor
The Greeks defeated the Persians in these two battles
The Greek word for city

```
S A L A M I S S T R S A I D I E H P
O K C E S S P A R T A P H E R I E E
I A R R P I E C A E U Q S O M R H R
N R T P O A L T H I N A H E I U M S
O Y A L R P R O A I A D I C K A S I
H A N A K L O T P R I L L K T T I A
T T E T E A L L H N K E Y S I O N N
H I H A K T O S I E S I K P N A O S
C D T I U A R K O S N P L S O A C R
I E A A Y E E L Q U E O T L S R K O
R S E I P A T H E N S U N I A S P P
E A N A I S E N N O P O L E P K L O
```

56

GREEK TEMPLE SCRAMBLE

1. This architectural order originated in the Greek towns of Asia Minor.   nocii   _ _ _ _ _
                                                         1

2. This principal beam was composed of long stone blocks. theacivarr   _ _ _ _ _ _ _ _ _ _
                                                         6

3. The Greek builders used these to join each block of the Parthenon with its vertically adjacent block.
loedsw   _ _ _ _ _ _
         8

4. This base formed the steps of a temple.
bestotaly   _ _ _ _ _ _ _ _ _
            4   11

5. The leaves of this flower were incorporated into the Corinthian column's capital.   hacustan   _ _ _ _ _ _ _ _
                                                         5

6. This sculptured ornament covered the end of each row of jointed roof tiles.   axefatin   _ _ _ _ _ _ _ _
                                                         3

7. This was the simplest of the three columns used by the Greeks.
rocdi   _ _ _ _ _
        7

8. This triangular space above either end of a Greek temple usually had sculptured reliefs.   mindteep   _ _ _ _ _ _ _ _
                                                         2

9. Greek temples had this below-ground foundation to provide extra strength.   beetatorse   _ _ _ _ _ _ _ _ _
                                                         9

10. Doric temples had a series of these separated by triglyphs.
posteem   _ _ _ _ _ _ _
          10   12

The Greek name for the temple chamber where the offerings of worshipers were placed: _ _ _ _ _ _ _ _ _ _ _ _
                                                 1 2 3 4 5 6 7 8 9 10 11 12

Unscramble the words to determine the answers to the clues. Then place each numbered letter on the corresponding blank line to discover the Greek name for the temple chamber where offerings were placed. The answers can be found in the articles on the Greek temple, pages 40–47, and on page 146.

GREECE VERSUS ROME

Can you match the Greek and Roman temple features on the right with the descriptions on the left? The answers can be found in the Greek versus Roman article, pages 48–51, and on page 146.

1. These qualities defined the Greek temple. _____

2. The Roman temple conveyed these qualities. _____

3. The Greeks positioned their temples facing east for this reason. _____

4. The Romans positioned their temples facing the marketplace for this reason. _____

5. This feature was the trademark of Greek design. _____

6. The Romans added this feature to their buildings to give them more space. _____

7. The Greeks used these three column orders. _____

8. The Romans added these two column orders. _____

9. These were the Greeks' building materials. _____

10. The Romans introduced these as building materials. _____

a. So the rising sun would light up the deity's statue

b. Post-and-lintel architecture

c. Doric, Ionic, and Corinthian

d. Vastness, magnificence, and strength

e. Stone or marble blocks

f. Simplicity, unity of form, and symmetry

g. To allow easy access to the temple

h. The curved arch

i. Concrete and broken pieces of stone

j. Tuscan and Composite

COMPANION

Topics for Comparison

1. Compare the Greek post-and-lintel style of architecture with the Roman use of the dome, arch, and vault. Compare the type of buildings each style can create. How do they differ in use and appearance?
2. Find out more about the Elgin Marbles. Who was Lord Elgin? Why was he in Athens? How did he gain possession of the Parthenon's metopes? Did he send any other artifacts back to England?
3. Compare and contrast the methods used by the ancient Greeks to "cement" together blocks of brick, stone, and/or marble with the methods used by masons and sculptors today. Include which methods you think require less care, which last longer, and which look better.
4. Walk slowly around your neighborhood or through your city or town and see how many houses and buildings have borrowed their designs from the architecture of Greece and Rome. Try to distinguish the Roman elements from the Greek. Compare and contrast modern plans and adaptations with those of the ancients.
5. As the fortunes of the ancients grew, they replaced wooden columns with stone or marble columns. Today we see both wooden and stone columns in cities throughout the United States. Compare the effects they create. Which do you prefer? Is one better in certain circumstances than the other? Elaborate.
6. Greek and Roman architectural styles reflect the personality of each country. Select a recently constructed building in your neighborhood, city, or state. How does it reflect the personality of the people who live there? Compare the ways in which ancient and modern architects accom-

plished this task. Did architects in one period do a better job than those in the other? Explain.

Suggestions for Writing Assignments

1. What was Thomas Jefferson's background? What was his training and schooling? Why did he favor the classical style, and how did he promote it?
2. The Acropolis was the pride of Athens and the barometer of its fortunes. The magnificence of the buildings erected on it and their subsequent ruin paralleled the rise and fall of the city. Elaborate on this statement and carry it into the present.
3. Benjamin Latrobe and Charles Bulfinch were architects in the United States known for their Greek Revival buildings. Who were these men? What buildings are credited to them? Who were other Greek Revival architects?
4. Elaborate on why the Greek Revival style was so readily adopted and adapted throughout the new United States after the Revolution.
5. Courthouses, customhouses, state capitol buildings, and banks were commonly built in the Greek Revival style. Why? Give examples.
6. The United States is not the only country where the Greek Revival style has been used. Give examples of buildings in other countries that were designed according to this style.

Further Activities

1. Look at the buildings in your city or town and the houses in your neighborhood. Find some with columns. Can you identify which are Doric, Ionic, and Corinthian? Are any of the columns Tuscan or Composite?

Did you find any pilasters?
2. Become an architect and design a temple. Have a reason for building the temple. Decide to whom you wish to dedicate your structure. (Pick some deity, legendary figure, hero, fictitious personality, or even yourself.) Tell which order of columns you would use and why. Design the scenes to be carved on the metopes or frieze. Remember, the theme of the designs must relate to the person or deity to whom you dedicate the temple.
3. The ancients had five main orders of architecture. If you were asked to create a sixth, what would it look like? Explain the reasons for your design.
4. The great building boom on the Acropolis coincided with the Golden Age of Athens and the rise of democracy. Research what was happening in other fields, such as drama and literature, at that time.

Topics for Debate

1. England should return the Elgin Marbles to Greece.
2. From the records of the ancients and from excavated finds, archaeologists and historians know and understand how the Parthenon was constructed and how it looked in the fifth century B.C. Should a full reconstruction of the Parthenon be initiated?

"I would rather have people ask why there is no statue of me than why there is one."

Marcus Cato (234–149 B.C.), Roman statesman

3 ANCIENT ARTISTS AND THEIR CRAFTS

CHAPTER

GREEK SCULPTURE

Greek sculpture is believed to have originated on the Mediterranean island of Crete. The theories developed there, together with the ideas of later sculptors in the Greek colonies of Asia Minor (present-day Turkey), gradually made their way to mainland Greece, where no sculpture existed in early times.

The first Greek statues were quite rigid in form. They stood facing front, hands at their sides, left foot forward. They had accentuated muscles, stylized hair, and a fixed smile.

In the latter part of the sixth century, it became the custom, especially in Athens, to fashion statues of victorious athletes. This practice afforded artists the opportunity to create something other than stiff religious statues. The athletes who trained daily for athletic contests were perfect models. As sculptors attempted to have their works resemble the human form more closely, the magnificence of the human body was glorified and humanism entered the realm of art.

Gradually, statues became less stereotyped in form. Athletes were shown in various positions, both at rest and in action. The Greek sculptor, however, was more concerned with the superb fitness of the human body than with the identifying features of a particular person. Therefore, although each sculptured body began to assume individual characteristics, its face did not.

During the Golden Age of Greece,

DISCOBOLO DI MIRONE

from about 460 to 400 B.C., the rulers of the Greek city-states, especially those in Athens, sought to beautify their cities, making them reflect the wealth, power, and prestige of the inhabitants. In Athens, more attention was given to artists and cultural activities than in any other city-state. Pericles, the outstanding Athenian statesman of this period, believed Athens had to be made worthy of its destiny. After Greece defeated the Persians at the Battle of Marathon in 490 B.C. and destroyed any hope the East had of conquering the countries of the West, a burst of artistic and cultural energy profoundly influenced not only the contemporary Mediterranean world but also succeeding generations.

Some of the greatest pieces ever sculptured were created during this period. One was the gigantic statue of the goddess Athena in the Parthenon, the work of the renowned Athenian sculptor Pheidias. Another was *The Discus Thrower* by Myron, another famous sculptor. The statue of Athena bore some resemblance to the art of the archaic period, whereas Myron's piece heralded the trend toward more realism. Myron was acknowledged as one of the first, if not the first, to represent moving figures of athletes and animals. In *The Discus Thrower,* he captured the moment just before the athlete hurls the discus, when every muscle is straining. One can almost feel the motion and the intensity of the action. This technique became one of the characteristics of the period.

In 1982, Nashville sculptor Alan LeQuire and several assistants began re-creating the ancient Greek sculptor Pheidias's statue of Athena. The replica stands almost 42 feet tall inside Nashville's Parthenon.

Opposite: A marble copy of the original bronze *Discus Thrower* stands today in Rome's Museo Nazionale delle Terme.

THE DEMISE OF GREEK SCULPTURE

As the decades passed, new trends emerged. Greek sculptors of the fourth century B.C. became more concerned with the reality of their immediate surroundings. The expression of emotion in art was emphasized.

One of the great masters of this period was Praxiteles, whose works were characterized by elegance of proportion and graceful beauty. Lysippos, the official sculptor of Alexander the Great, also ranked among the best of the age. One of the most famous pieces of this later period was the Pergamon[1] Frieze, with its statue *The Dying Gaul* (also called, though incorrectly, *The Dying Gladiator*). Increased movement and heightened expression became the chief characteristics of the Hellenistic[2] style, the name given to the art, history, and culture of Greece following the conquests of Alexander the Great.

Unfortunately, the quality of sculptured pieces gradually deteriorated as the artists' ingenuity diminished. Many sculptors produced reproductions of earlier masterpieces instead of creating their own works. Creativity and originality seemed lost as Greece's Golden Age faded. In the previous centuries, sculptors had been divided into various schools of thought, and their works reflected this. Later artists either copied a particular piece exactly or based their work on the rules and beliefs of a certain school.

One of the most famous schools was the Pergamene School. The well-known group composition known as *Laocoön and His Sons*[3] belongs to this school. In his novel *A Christmas Carol*, the English author Charles Dickens (1812–1870) compared the long comforter (scarf) wrapped around Bob Cratchit's neck to the serpents encircling Laocoön's body.

The later Greeks were not the only ones to copy

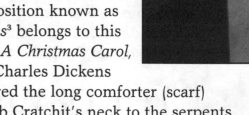

---

1. Pergamon was a flourishing Greek city-state in Asia Minor from 282 to 133 B.C. To commemorate Pergamon's victory over the invading Gauls (sometime before 230 B.C.), the king of Pergamon commissioned a triumphal monument that included *The Dying Gaul.*

2. The Greeks referred to themselves as the Hellenes, a derivative of Hellen, Zeus's son and the father of the mythical founders of the original four tribes that inhabited Greece.

3. In the great Trojan War, Laocoön was a Trojan who counseled his countrymen not to accept the Greeks' gift of an enormous wooden horse. The gods who favored the Greeks sent serpents from the deep sea to coil themselves around Laocoön and his sons and kill them. The Trojans accepted the gift and were defeated by the Greek soldiers hiding inside.

their ancestors' masterpieces. As Rome came in contact with the art of other nations, the style it most readily adopted was that of Greece. Rome's sculptors produced numerous excellent copies of famous Greek works. Some were for private citizens, others to adorn public buildings.

Although the creativity and originality of the earlier Greek artists had been lost, their works had a great influence on the Roman world. During the Renaissance and the centuries that followed, Hellenism, with its superb naturalistic portrayal of the human form, became the inspiration for European artists and sculptors.

Barely able to support himself on one arm, *The Dying Gaul* appears bent and in pain as blood spurts from his wounded right side. The twisted collar around his neck, the mustache, and the hair style suggest he is a Gaul.

ENDANGERED SCULPTURES

Many original classical sculptures were destroyed when what they represented no longer was in fashion or when new rulers sought to suppress the past. Others were mutilated and maimed by those who needed pieces of marble, stone, and gold for new statues. The few that remain owe their survival primarily to accidental burial in collapsed buildings.

Some statues, such as *Hermes* of Praxiteles and *Venus de Milo*,[1] were hidden and worshiped in secret by members of various religious sects. Others, because of their prominent position in a public square or building, were regarded with reverence and superstition. An example is the equestrian statue of the Roman emperor Marcus Aurelius (A.D. 121–180) on Rome's Capitoline Hill. During the Middle Ages and the rise of Christianity, the rider was believed, incorrectly, to be Constantine, the Roman emperor who in 313 granted Christians the right to practice their religion without fear of persecution. For this reason, the statue was never marred or disfigured.

1. Praxiteles and Milo were the ancient sculptors of these statues.

In 1537, when the Italian sculptor and painter Michaelangelo (1475–1564) was designing the Piazza del Campidoglio on the Capitoline Hill, the bronze equestrian statue of Marcus Aurelius became the focal point of the square's design. The statue is now behind glass in the hill's museum to protect it from pollution, weather, and vandalism.

ROMAN SCULPTURE

The Romans recognized the Greeks as master sculptors. Rome's conquest of Corinth, the last Greek stronghold, in 146 B.C. ushered in an age of wholesale adoption of Greek sculptural ideas and techniques. It also signaled the end of creativity and originality among the Greeks, who realized that the Romans sought the works of the early Greek masters.

In 27 B.C., Octavius Caesar, later known as Augustus, was declared the leader of the Roman world. His rule marked the beginning of the Golden Age of Rome. Octavius's determination to beautify Rome and make the city worthy of being the capital of the world made Rome a paradise for artists and sculptors. Because Greek work was especially prized, Greek artisans flocked to Rome.

Although thousands of Greek statues had been imported prior to this period to adorn Roman homes, temples, and public buildings, thousands more were imported now. In addition, numerous

Above: Thousands of sarcophagi, each with its own unique reliefs and symbolism, have been uncovered among ancient ruins. This one dates to the 2nd or 3rd century A.D. and is housed in the Archaeology Museum in Alexandria, Egypt. **Right:** Discovered in Rome in 1506, centuries after its creation, the statue of Laocoön and his two sons writhing in pain as snakes encircle their limbs exemplifies the style of sculpture known as Hellenistic.

copies of Greek statues were made. To display these works of art, semicircular or rectangular niches and recessed areas in the walls of buildings became the fashion. Architects often fronted these areas with a row of columns or used side columns and a pediment to "outline" the area.

Most of the material written about Greek and Roman sculpture emphasizes the tremendous legacy of the Greek sculptors, and the work of Roman sculptors often is overlooked. The Romans, however, were not pure imitators. They did make contributions to sculpture.

A widely practiced custom among the Romans was the making of wax masks of dead family members. These masks were carefully preserved and treasured. Roman statues and busts reflected this practice, as faces became uncompromisingly realistic. No attempt

In A.D. 113, the Roman emperor Trajan erected a 100-foot column in the Forum at Rome to commemorate his successful campaigns in Dacia (present-day north-central and western Rumania). **Inset:** Carved on the spiral band that winds for 215 yards along the column are scenes illustrating Trajan's march from Rome and his victory over the Dacians.

was made to flatter a subject by omitting a disfiguring mark or blemish. The Roman sculptor's golden rule was faithfulness to life, and in the field of lifelike portraits, Roman artists surpassed all others.

The Romans also excelled in the relief work they fashioned to decorate sarcophagi (large stone boxes similar to our coffins). Since burial within the walls of a Roman city was forbidden, the Romans built mausoleums to house their dead. Often the remains of a deceased individual were placed in a sarcophagus, the sides of which were covered with low-relief sculptured panels.

At first, the scenes on these panels were allegorical and mythical. However, as Rome extended its rule around the Mediterranean world, the depiction of contemporary events, such as battles and triumphal marches, came into vogue. The distinguishing char-

GREEK VERSUS ROMAN SCULPTURE

The Greeks were concerned with the accurate treatment of the body and muscle structure; the Romans concentrated on facial features. The portrayal of an individual's distinguishing characteristics was so important to the Romans that ready-made statue bodies were mass-produced and available for sale. A Roman citizen would purchase such a statue and then commission a sculptor to chisel the desired head and face before screwing it into the body.

Whereas the Greeks believed that simplicity was an essential aspect of beauty, the Romans enjoyed adding superfluous decorations wherever possible. As a result, they developed the art of scrollwork and various floral and foliage designs for use on their private and public buildings.

Both Greek and Roman sculptors have influenced the art of the Western world, but the works of the two groups should not be classified together as classical sculpture. Rather, each should be appreciated for its own merits and contributions.

acteristic of this work was its realistic quality. Soon sculptors were commissioned to fashion sculptured panels not only for sarcophagi but also for altars, triumphal arches, and other public monuments.

In later years, when columns were erected in recognition of outstanding achievements, sculptors were occasionally commissioned to depict scenes commemorating the event in circular fashion on the column itself. The Roman emperor Trajan's column in the Roman forum is perhaps the best existing example.

Another Roman contribution to sculpture was the equestrian statue. Throughout the Roman world, these mounted sculptures immortalized Roman heroes. The tradition survives in the statues we see adorning public gardens and buildings of the twentieth century.

ART IN ANCIENT GREECE

Greece's mountainous terrain and the three seas (Mediterranean, Ionian, and Aegean) that surround it tended to isolate the early city-states, but these geographic features also fostered a respect for nature and life. A religious people, the ancient Greeks believed that everyone should give thanks to the immortal gods for the gift of life. Building a magnificent temple was one way of doing this. Creating reproductions of human life was another.

Greek painting as art is said to have begun with the fifth-century B.C. painter Polygnotos. Before this period, Greek understanding of botany and human anatomy was limited. Hence, features and posture were quite severe and unrealistic. Polygnotos is credited with introducing more realistic features. Lifelike representations of muscles and joints followed. Using the descriptions and observations of nature and the animal kingdom made by the fourth-century B.C. Greek philosopher Aristotle and his followers, the Greeks gradually mastered the art of portraying the human form artistically.

Because very few Greek paintings survived the centuries, much of our knowledge about Greek art comes from the works of Roman writers. (The Romans imported thousands of pieces of Greek art.) For example, Roman authors tell us that the Greeks generally used only a few colors in their art. In addition, early designs often were simple, repeated patterns. As far as materials, Greek painters used a variety of brushes for wall and easel paintings. The coarser type was made of bristles, the finer of close-textured sponge. A large piece of sponge served as both an eraser and a means of washing out the brush.

The ancient Greeks enjoyed fresco painting, a

method that involved painting on freshly spread plaster before it dried. First, a wet surface was carefully prepared. Mortar remains damp longer and does not require rewetting each day if it is laid thickly, so a thick layer of sand mortar and marble stucco was the norm. The painter used a brush and water colors. The water in the paint and the water in the mortar combined to give added strength and durability to the painting. Since varnish as a protective surface was unknown, folding doors were sometimes constructed to cover and guard a painting.

Another technique of painting discovered during the fifth century B.C. but not really developed until the fourth century was the encaustic method. Paintings of this type have not survived, and ancient accounts of them are sketchy. Essentially, the artist used colored wax to create a scene on stucco. Historians believe that the Greeks melted the wax and then kept it in a pot. When the wax had solidified, the design was polished (rubbed with a wax candle), then cleaned with a linen cloth. Later, the colors of the picture were fixed by passing a hot blend of wax, stucco, and/or ashes over the design. This method, though slow and tedious, produced works that were durable and whose colors were bright and attractive.

In 1977, several royal tombs (one thought to be that of Philip II, the father of Alexander the Great) were discovered at Vergina, Greece. This exciting find has yielded numerous works of art. Today archaeologists and historians continue to excavate the area, seeking more information about the methods and styles of the ancient Greek painters.

PARRHASIOS'S CURTAIN

Paintings to deceive the eye seemed to be the goal of two fifth-century B.C. Greek painters named Parrhasios and Zeuxis. Contemporaries, they knew each other well. Parrhasios hailed from the Greek colony of Ephesos in Asia Minor and Zeuxis from the Greek colony of Herakleia in southern Italy. Both were master artists, famed for their accurate, detailed, and extremely realistic scenes.

According to the ancient Greeks, Parrhasios and Zeuxis once challenged each other to a contest. The heated debates that had arisen between their loyal followers had forced them to find some means of determining which one was better. Neither rejoiced at the opportunity, but each took it very seriously and spent weeks hidden away in his studio drafting and redrafting his entry.

Finally, the day of the contest arrived. Hundreds of followers waited outside the great room that had been prepared for the event. Inside, Parrhasios and Zeuxis waited motionless and expressionless, neither one betraying his intense anticipation. Beside each was his entry, covered with its own curtain and bound by a gold cord.

When the room could hold no more spectators, the doors were closed. The silence was deafening.

"You, my friend," said Parrhasios, "may go first."

Zeuxis nodded. Before pulling the gold cord to draw back the curtain covering his painting, Zeuxis opened a cage that he had brought with him and set loose a small flock of birds. Then, as the curtain fell, the crowd gasped. Was it a painting or a table set with a bowl of grapes? Even the birds seemed to stop midway in flight. Before anyone could speak, the birds flew straight toward the grapes and began to nibble. But all they tasted was paint. Zeuxis's followers applauded and cheered their hero.

"Your turn, Parrhasios," Zeuxis said.

Parrhasios bowed slightly. He raised his hand to pull the gold cord, then stopped with his arm in midair. He hesitated and turned to Zeuxis.

"My dear friend, Zeuxis," he said, "would you do the honor of uncovering my painting?"

FROM PAUSANIAS'S GUIDE TO GREECE

Pausanias, a second-century A.D. Greek traveler and writer, described many of the paintings he saw. In Volume I, Book X, of his *Guide to Greece,* Pausanias tells of a building whose walls had been painted by Polygnotos:

Above Kassotis [a spring in central Greece near Delphi] is a building with paintings by Polygnotos.... The Delphians call it the Club-House because this is where they met in ancient times both for storytelling and for serious conversations.... As you enter the building, a painting depicts the fall of Troy and the Greeks as they sailed away.... In another scene, Polygnotos painted Nestor [a Greek king] with a hat on his head and a spear in his hand; there is also a horse which is about to roll in the sand; the beach comes as far as the horse and you can even see the pebbles.... Such is the beauty of the painting.

"Most certainly!" Zeuxis replied, and without a moment's hesitation, he reached out his hand to pull the cord. But there was no cord. The curtain and the gold cord were Parrhasios's entry.

After a long silence, Zeuxis finally regained his composure. "Congratulations, my friend," he said. "Certainly you have won. I deceived only the birds; you deceived me."

ROMAN ART

Roman painting was generally confined to the decoration of the interior walls of buildings. The subjects varied from mythological topics to scenes of daily life. After Rome's conquest of Greece in 146 B.C., Greek works of art found a ready and eager market in Rome. Greek artists were in great demand, and Roman artists imitated their ideas.

The Romans used the fresco method of painting. Roman writers tell us that artists painted on a base consisting of three layers of sand mortar followed by two or three layers of marble mortar. (The Romans understood the importance of thick mortar, just as the Greeks had.) The artists then smoothed and flattened the surface by rubbing a piece of wood across it. Roman artists used brushes and water colors. The water in the paints combined with the water and lime in the mortar to make the wall and the painting one unit. This process did not work with certain colors, however, and other binding substances, such as milk, were used.

Four of the world's best-known paintings were buried during the A.D. 79 eruption of Mount Vesuvius. Three were discovered in Pompeii: *Venus Marina* (also called *Venus on the Half Shell*), *Garden Scene in the House of Venus Marina,* and *Portrait of a Husband and Wife.* A fourth painting, *The Centaur Chiron Trains Young Achilles in the Art of Music,* was found in Herculaneum.

Top: From August 24 to 26, A.D. 79, Mount Vesuvius erupted, destroying many surrounding towns, including Pompeii. Centuries later, treasure hunters haphazardly dug down into the buried city, seeking artifacts to adorn their homes and to sell. In 1860, the new director of the site reorganized the work being done there and set rules for orderly, scientific excavations. **Below:** Roman families worshiped special personal deities whom they believed protected and guarded their homes. A small shrine called a *lararium,* which usually resembled the façade of a temple, was erected near the entrance. Statues or figures painted directly on the wall represented the deities. Pictures of snakes were common, as they were considered good luck.

These frescoes and others have provided some of the best illustrations of ancient mythology. In addition, many of the landscape paintings are serenely beautiful. Since the excavations began in the 1700s, artists throughout the world have painted their interpretations of these ancient scenes.

THE FOUR STYLES OF ROMAN PAINTING

The First Style was the simplest, with little color and few pictures. Sometimes the wall was divided by lines or geometric patterns of another color.

The Second Style incorporated pictures, architectural landscapes, and vistas into its design. Figures also were introduced.

The Third Style was much more elaborate. A landscape scene was used as a backdrop, and a single figure or group of figures was painted in the foreground. Both the Second and Third styles added visually to the dimensions of the house or building by giving the viewer the impression that he or she was looking at a serene outdoor scene.

The Fourth Style was flamboyant and often impressionistic. The architectural vistas of the Second Style were reintroduced, and almost every part of the frame was filled with drawings of figures, statuary, and even landscape scenes.

GREEK VERSUS ROMAN ART

Greek paintings are easily distinguished from their Roman counterparts. The Greeks treated daily life ideally and at times quite unrealistically. All was fresh, simple, and beautiful. In contrast, the Romans were concerned with the daily life of the craftsmen. Market scenes were common. The Roman artists excelled in portraiture, and their death masks were very realistic.

THE GREEK POTTER

The growth and advancement of Greek civilization can be traced through a study of Greek vases. In very ancient times, gourds were hollowed out to serve as containers. After the properties of clay became better understood, Greek potters began to fashion clay pots, using gourds as models. Gradually, clay was used to fashion all types of jars, jugs, and drinking vessels. Therefore, it is not surprising that thousands of these vessels have survived the centuries, many completely intact.

Vessels were shaped according to the intended use. The designs were functional and practical, with nothing unnecessary added. Rather than search for new and different shapes, Greek potters preferred to perfect existing designs until a graceful balance between functionalism and beauty was achieved.

Deposits of clay, a product of the continued weathering and erosion of the earth's surface, were, and still are, found in abundance throughout Greece. Potters mixed various clays to obtain a certain color or special characteristics. (Clays differ in color and properties, and not all are suitable for making pottery.) The deposits found in the area around Corinth, in central Greece, were whitish in color. The clay found in eastern Greece, in the area called Attica, was reddish brown due to the presence of iron.

"Raw" clay had to be purified, as it came out of the quarry mixed with sand, small stones, decayed vegetable matter, and other foreign materials. To do this, workers combined the clay with water and then put the mixture in a huge basin. The heavier impurities settled to the bottom, and the clay, which rose to the surface, was pumped into another basin. This process was repeated until the workers deemed the clay fine enough to use for pottery. The type of vessel to be made dictated the degree of purity required — the more delicate the vessel, the finer the clay.

Once the clay was considered pure enough, it was allowed to set for several months. This was necessary for the clay to retain its shape during molding.

After the setting period, the potter beat the clay to obtain a smooth consistency and to remove air bubbles. The potter then placed a ball of clay on his rotating wheel. (The potter's wheel is believed to have been invented in Asia Minor sometime around 3000 B.C.) Worked by a helper's hand (foot-operated wheels were unknown to the ancients), the wheel allowed the potter to use both hands in shaping the clay. The rotation of the wheel created a momentum that transferred the energy to the clay, making the latter more pliable and easier to shape.

Once the potter had obtained the desired form, he left the clay to dry. When the vessel was dry, the potter placed it on the wheel a second time and removed any unwanted clay with metal, bone, or wooden tools. He then smoothed the surface with a wet sponge and added handles, feet, and pedestals. To remove the vessel from the wheel, the potter pulled a wire or cord under the clay as it turned on the wheel.

Very large containers were made in sections and then joined together so skillfully with wet clay that the joints were invisible. Completed vases were kept in a damp room until they were ready to be decorated and fired in a special oven called a kiln.

The technique of firing dried clay in a kiln to make it a hard, useful material had been discovered thousands of years earlier, but the process had been greatly refined over the centuries. The Greek kiln had two areas, one in which the potter stacked his pots and the other in which the fire burned. At the top of the kiln was a vent hole or chimney, which was covered at certain times during the firing process. Each kiln also had a door and a spy hole so that the potter could monitor the firing process. To check their work, potters used test pieces with holes in them. The potter could easily remove a test piece with a hooked stick to check whether it was "done."

The production of pottery was one of Greece's most active industries. Greek potters were considered the best in ancient times, and Greek vases were exported to communities throughout the Mediterranean world. Many twentieth-century potters and interior decorators have been inspired by the simple beauty of ancient Greek vases.

DECORATING A GREEK VASE

In very ancient times, potters rarely decorated their products. Gradually, however, incised lines and techniques such as pinching the rim of a vessel to create a decorative touch were introduced. Potters also realized that the method of firing affected the color of red clay. If the fire burned freely, the final product was buff-red. If the fire was smothered, it was gray-black.

As potters became more daring, they began to fashion vases covered with geometric designs. Later, human and animal figures were added. Soon potters began to treat vases as painters use canvases and drew scenes depicting the deities and their exploits, Greek heroes, military expeditions, and daily life.

Most Greek vases are classified according to the color of the figures. In the earlier black-figured style, the painter used a brush to paint black-enamel figures on the vase. Details were added by incising lines in the silhouette with a small, pointed instrument that cut through the enamel to the clay body of the vase.

In the more advanced red-figured style, the painter outlined the figures in silhouette and covered the rest of the vase with black enamel. This method gradually superseded others, as it enhanced the beauty of the figures. Details were applied with a brush rather than using the difficult process of incising lines.

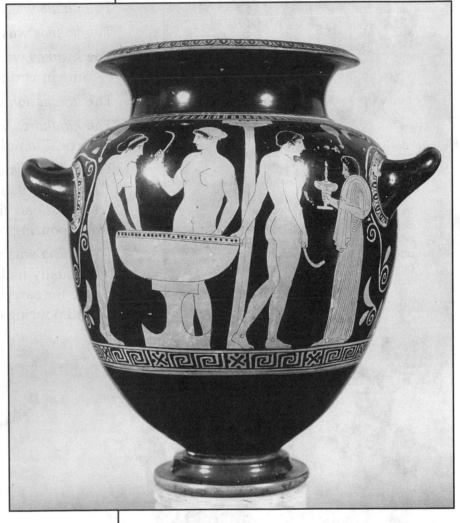

The *stamnos* held wine or oil.

The *amphora* was one of the most commonly used jars. It was either buried halfway in the ground or set slanting against the wall. Store owners used amphorae to keep honey and wine drawn from large, fermenting vats.

The Greek potter fashioned a great variety of vases, each with its own specific use. The silhouettes here illustrate some of the vessels made.

The *phiale* was a saucer-shaped drinking vessel.

The *holmos* was a drinking vessel.

The *kyathos* was used to ladle or pour out wine and came in various sizes to hold specific amounts.

The *karchesion* was a drinking vessel.

The *kantharos* was a drinking vessel with two high vertical handles.

The *kalpis* was used for drawing and holding water. It usually had three handles—a small one on each side for carrying water and another for drawing and pouring out water.

The *hydria* was used for drawing and holding water. It usually had three handles—a small one on each side for carrying water and another for drawing and pouring out water.

The *krater* was used to mix wine with water at meals. Sometimes it had a stand to support its rounded, pointed, or pedestaled bottom.

TELLS ALL

The *pelike* was used for storage.

The *kelebe* was used for storage and for mixing wine and water.

The *askos* resembled a goatskin and was used for transporting wine.

The *legoena* was hung as a sign in front of wine shops and was put before guests at table.

The *alabastron* was used for fragrant ointments. Its narrow neck allowed the liquid to run out in drops. Its round bottom required a stand for support.

The *aryballos* held oil used in anointing the dead. Greek women also used it to keep perfumes and oils. Its narrow neck allowed the liquid to run out in drops.

The *bombylios* was a drinking vessel with a very narrow mouth.

The *lekane* was a storage vessel.

The *oinochoe* was a wine container that took its shape from that of wineskins—the leather bags country folk used to store wine and oil.

The *kylix* (left and below) was a shallow drinking vessel that usually had a pedestaled foot.

The *lekythos* held oil used in anointing the dead. Greek women also used it to keep perfumes and oils. Its narrow neck allowed the liquid to run out in drops.

DESIGN A MOSAIC

For thousands of years, artists and craftspeople have used pebbles, tiny pieces of stone or marble, and, in some areas, glass to create pictures on flat surfaces such as floors and walls. These pictures are called mosaics. Some mosaics are quite simple; others are extremely intricate and detailed.

Greek craftsmen of the fifth century B.C. refined the art of making mosaics. Using white and black pebbles, all similar in size, they created various floor designs. For variety, fourth-century B.C. Greeks added red and green painted pebbles. Soon thereafter, cut pieces of stone or marble were used. Craftsmen of the Hellenistic period introduced glass, a refinement that added color and allowed mosaics to be used as windows or on walls.

The Romans loved to decorate their floors with mosaics. Many have been uncovered, still intact, at excavation sights throughout the ancient Roman world.

The directions given here are for a mosaic made out of paper. However, if you live in an area where small, round pebbles can be found in abundance, you might want to try making a mosaic out of pebbles.

– illustrated by Annette Cate

80

You Need

pencil

plain white paper

sand or dirt (enough to fill the box bottom to a depth of 1 inch)

box bottom with sides about 2 inches high (The best type of box is one that was used as the packing box for an appliance such as a refrigerator, stove, or washing machine. Appliance box bottoms usually have a metal tape that holds the cardboard sides in place. This makes a perfect mosaic bed. Call ahead to an appliance store in your area and ask them to save one for you.)

glue

construction paper in a variety of colors

corrugated cardboard (Call ahead to a supermarket and ask them to save you several empty packing boxes. Before beginning the project, cut the sides to the size needed for your mosaic.)

scissors

1. Make a pencil design of your mosaic on the white paper. Mark which sections or pieces will be which color.

2. Spread the sand or dirt evenly on the box bottom.

3. With the tip of your pencil, trace your mosaic design in the sand or dirt.

4. Glue each piece of construction paper to a piece of corrugated cardboard. Set the pieces aside until the glue is dry.

5. Cut the pieces of corrugated cardboard and construction paper into squares, diamonds, rectangles, triangles, half-moons, and circles. For greater ease when fashioning your mosaic, do not cut the pieces too small. Also, leave larger pieces of each color uncut so that when you need a particular shape as you fashion your mosaic, you will be able to custom-cut that piece.

6. Carefully arrange the cut pieces, one at a time, on top of your design. Press each piece slightly into the sand or dirt.

7. As you fill in the design, you will need to custom-cut pieces to fit. First measure each space, then cut the required piece out of the appropriate colored paper. Fill in every empty space in this manner.

8. Check to see if you need to make any changes in the finished design. If not, congratulations! You have just completed a mosaic.

81

A GREEK AND ROMAN MATCH

Match each clue with the appropriate phrase. The answers can be found in the articles on Greek and Roman sculpture, pages 62–69, and on page 149.

1. Greek sculpture was believed to have originated here. _____
2. The Greeks strongly believed that this was an essential aspect of beauty.

_____
3. Work by master Athenian sculptor Myron. _____
4. Two characteristics of early Greek sculpture. _____
5. This sculptured work belongs to the Pergamene School.

_____
6. Roman sculptors concentrated on portraying these very realistically. _____
7. One of Rome's contributions to the world of sculpture.

_____
8. The Roman sculptor's golden rule. _____
9. During his rule, Rome was a sculptors' paradise. _____
10. The Roman statue of this person survived the Middle Ages because it was incorrectly thought to represent Constantine the Great. _____

a. *Laocoön and His Sons*
b. Faithfulness to life
c. Facial features
d. Mediterranean island of Crete
e. Octavius Caesar
f. *The Discus Thrower*
g. Simplicity
h. Roman emperor Marcus Aurelius
i. Standing facing front, stylized hair
j. Equestrian statue

CROSSWORD PUZZLE

ACROSS

1. Greek philosopher
4. Fifth-century B.C. Greek painter
6. Romans used this to smooth and flatten fresco paintings
7. In the Third Style of Roman painting, this type of scene was the usual backdrop
11. A painting of the Centaur Chiron was uncovered here
13. Greeks liked this type of painting
14. This sea borders Greece
17. His grapes were so real they fooled the birds
18. This sea borders Greece
21. Roman artists excelled in this field
23. They have told us most of what we know about Greek painting
24. *Venus on the Half Shell* was uncovered here
25. Roman artists often incorporated scenes of this area into their paintings

DOWN

2. Fine Greek brushes were made of this
3. A technique Greek painters used most in the fourth century
4. His painting of a curtain was so real it fooled another painter
5. Type of cloth Greeks used to clean design painted by the encaustic method
8. These landscapes were common to the Second Style of Roman painting
9. In the encaustic method, the Greeks used this to polish their designs (two words)
10. To protect paintings, the Greeks sometimes used these
12. Greek painters knew that a thick layer of this was best for fresco painting
15. This sea borders Greece
16. Works of art were found in tombs here
19. Greek painters used this as an eraser
20. Century (B.C.) when Greek painting began
22. Number of styles of Roman painting

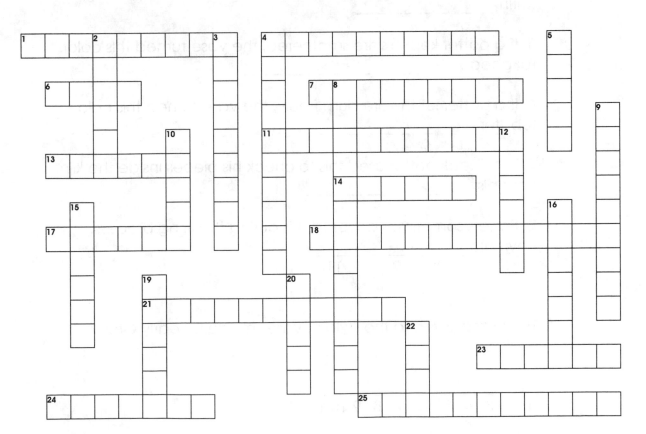

The answers can be found in the articles on Greek and Roman art, pages 70–74, and on page 149.

A POTTER'S SCRAMBLE

Unscramble the eight jumbled words to determine the answers to the clues. Then place the numbered letters on the corresponding blank lines to discover the name given to the vases made by early Greek potters. The answers can be found in the articles on Greek pottery, pages 75–79, and on page 149.

1. Greek potters used these as their models.
dusgor _ _ _ _ _ _
         8   10

2. The ancients used this material to make storage containers.
alyc _ _ _ _
       4

3. This is a potter's oven.
nilk _ _ _ _
       5

4. This process was used to bake the clay.
rgifin _ _ _ _ _ _
         6

5. If a potter kept his fire smothered, the vase turned this color.
rakgbcaly _ _ _ _ - _ _ _ _ _
            3   1

6. If a potter let the fire burn freely, the vase turned this color.
fubdfer _ _ _ _ - _ _ _
          9   12

7. The Greek potter used this to check his pieces inside the kiln.
heyopls _ _ _ _ _ _ _
                  2

8. Potters sometimes covered this during the firing process.
heymnic _ _ _ _ _ _ _
          7   11

The name given to the style of vases made by early Greek potters:

_ _ _ _ _ - _ _ _ _ _ _ _
1 2 3 4 5   6 7 8 9 10 11 12

COMPANION 3

Topics for Comparison

1. Roman artists are considered masters at realism. Yet the Greek tale of Zeuxis and Parrhasios points to a desire for incredible realism. Compare the differences between the Greeks' approach toward realism and the Romans' approach.

2. Both Greece and Rome experienced a Golden Age. Yet this period when the arts flourished affected the nations differently. Compare and contrast the styles and tendencies of the Golden Age artists of both nations.

3. A Roman could walk into a shop, buy a headless statue, and then have a head fashioned. An ancient Greek would have scoffed at this. Compare and contrast these two lines of thought.

4. Compare the four styles of Roman wall painting. What do you think the purpose of each was? Which do you prefer? Why?

5. The Romans marked their accomplishments with monuments in the capital city of Rome. Find a detailed picture book of Washington, D.C. Describe the monuments we have used to decorate our capital and the significant events they commemorate.

Suggestions for Writing Assignments

1. Greek sculpture reflects Greece's political fortunes. Relate Greek sculpture to the early period of Greece's history, the rise of democracy and the Golden Age, and Greece's conquest by Rome.

2. Many ancient sculptural monuments were destroyed by new rulers who came to power. This pattern has continued throughout history. After the fall of the Berlin Wall in Germany and the breakup of the Soviet Union in the early 1990s, the wall and many of the statues of former rulers were destroyed. Give other examples of this phenomenon.

Explain why this behavior occurs. What satisfaction do the "destroyers" get from acting this way?

3. Roman artists were realists. A subject's face was portrayed as is. What does this reflect about the thinking of the Romans?

4. Greek artists were idealists. The body's proportions and superb form were stressed. What does this reflect about the thinking of the Greeks?

5. The Greeks were very concerned with beauty and attempted to express it in all their creations. Yet the Greeks never added any unnecessary decorations. Why?

6. Throughout the Western world, equestrian statues, modeled after those fashioned by the ancient Romans, have been erected to honor national and military heroes. Research some modern examples of such statues.

7. Athens and Sparta were rival Greek city-states. Many of Greece's most famous architects, artists, sculptors, and philosophers were Athenians. Sparta left no traces of cultural achievements. Could the fact that Athens promoted a democratic form of government and Sparta an aristocratic form of government have contributed to the cultural growth and achievement (or lack thereof) in each city-state?

Further Activities

1. Become a potter and design a vase. (You can fashion your vase out of modeling clay or draw the design on paper.) First decide what its use will be. Then design the style so that you can color it authentically. After your work is complete, test your design by asking your family, friends, or classmates to guess the purpose for which your vase could be used.

2. Visit an art museum that houses a collection of Greek vases. Study the shapes. Can you identify the uses before reading the plates? Can you

identify the style? Which style do you prefer: red-figured or black-figured? Why?

3. Visit the classical sculpture wing of an art museum near you. Compare the Greek and Roman statues. How do they differ?

4. Go to the library and take out a book on Pompeii. Look for one that has color reproductions of the rooms that have been uncovered. Can you identify the styles used to decorate the walls?

5. Try to find a book that has illustrations of the famous paintings discovered during the excavations of Pompeii and Herculaneum. (Many books on the history of art include paintings from these two ancient cities.)

6. If there is a potter or a pottery-making factory near you, call and ask to visit. See how pottery is made today. Are there any ways in which modern methods resemble ancient techniques? (Another suggestion: If you live near a historical site that replicates early American life, visit the potter at the site to compare techniques.)

Topics for Debate

1. Rome conquered Greece on the battlefield, but Greece conquered Rome in the field of art and sculpture.

2. Greece's defeat at the hands of the Romans contributed more to the decline of originality in Greek sculpture than did the Romans' desire for copies of the fifth-century master sculptors' works.

3. According to the ancient Greeks, Parrhasios won the art contest, but Zeuxis should have been named the winner. Parrhasios deceived only the sense of sight. Zeuxis deceived two senses—sight and smell.

"Compare with such indispensable structures as these aqueducts which carry so many waters the idle pyramids or the useless, although famous, works of the Greeks."

Frontinus, 1st-century A.D. Roman water commissioner

CHAPTER 4
ROME'S INGENIOUS ENGINEERS

The buildings mentioned in this chapter are in chronological order according to the date of the beginning of their construction.

THE TIMELESS VIA APPIA

If stones could speak, those along the Via Appia (Appian Way) would give the world a fascinating account of more than two thousand years of history. In ancient times, those stones withstood the feet of triumphant Roman soldiers and proud but dejected captives from Europe, Asia, and Africa. Similarly, in the twentieth century, they have felt the feet of soldiers from many nations fighting in both world wars and statesmen journeying to Rome for international meetings.

Named for Appius Claudius Caecus, the Roman censor who commissioned its construction about 312 B.C., the Via Appia was probably the first great Roman road to be built. As the Roman world expanded, Rome's leaders recognized the need for a reliable system of communication between the seat of government in Rome and the far-flung provinces. An international road system was their answer. The implementation of this plan began with the Via Appia, which measured approximately three hundred fifty miles in length, and continued until paved roads, many of which are still used today, crisscrossed the entire Roman Empire.

These roads made possible a great exchange of ideas, customs, and commercial products and fostered a spirit of unity among Rome's subjects. Along the Via Appia and other main roads, posting houses with fresh teams of horses and vehicles and resting stations or inns were available.

Today a walk along the Via Appia transports visitors back across the centuries to the time of the ancient Romans. The way is lined with the ruins of ancient monuments, tombstones, and mausoleums. (Burial within the city walls was prohibited in ancient Rome.) The Italian composer Ottorino Respighi (1879–1936) was so moved by this area that he wrote a symphonic piece titled *The Pines of Rome.* The fourth movement, called "Pines of the Appian Way," embodies his vision of the glories of Rome. As the trumpets blare and the orchestral forces gather strength into a mighty crescendo (increase in volume of sound), every listener can feel the tread of the Roman soldiers' feet as they accompany their general in the traditional triumphal march along the Appian Way to the Capitoline Hill in the center of Rome.

The Via Appia is still in such good condition that present-day Italian road engineers have followed the path of the old Roman road, used its foundations to strengthen their own roads, and left various sections untouched in silent testimony to the ancient Romans.

As 20th-century Romans zoom along the Appian Way, the monuments and ruins along the road remind them of their illustrious past.

THE ROMAN AQUEDUCT

The maintenance of a steady water supply is a priority for every government. When Rome's leaders realized that the Tiber River and its nearby streams did not supply enough water to meet the city's increasing needs, Roman architects were ordered to develop a reliable and efficient method of importing water.

The first Roman aqueduct was built in 312 B.C. Named the Appia in honor of Appius Claudius Caecus, the public official in charge of public works at the time, this structure was approximately eleven miles long, with its greater portion laid underground. Forty years later, another aqueduct, the Anio, was built.

As Rome continued to grow in power and size,

more structures were needed to transport water from the springs and streams in Italy's interior. In 144 B.C., the Marcia was begun. This aqueduct stretched across more than sixty miles of Italian countryside and traveled above ground as it carried its exceptionally cold and sparkling water to the capital city. It has been calculated that the Marcia could supply Rome with forty million gallons of water every day.

By the end of the first century A.D., nine aqueducts covering about three hundred miles entered Rome, with a daily input of more than two hundred thousand gallons of water. In A.D. 97, Julius Frontinus assumed the position of *curator aquarum* (caretaker of the waters, or water commissioner). Frontinus greatly improved this magnificent engineering system. He had detailed plans made of each aqueduct, especially of those sites that required extra care. His work *About the Aqueducts of the City of Rome* has helped historians and archaeologists understand the construction, size, and capacity of the Roman water system.

Today the term "aqueduct" brings to mind the image of a massive but graceful double- or triple-tiered series of arches spanning a valley. However, such arched bridges were rare, for they were very expensive to build. The Romans preferred to run the aqueducts along the ground or under the ground. Once the water reached Rome, it was diverted to areas such as the great public baths, businesses requiring water (such as cleaners and tanners), fountains (both drinking and ornamental), and arenas in which *naumachiae* (mock naval battles) were held.

The Romans' development of the arch and a type of cement that hardens and sets underwater allowed them to build these aqueducts. Many are still in use today, as are the ancient reservoirs, which aid farmers in irrigating their fields.

Under the Roman emperor Augustus (27 B.C.–A.D.14), the aqueduct known today as the Pont du Gard (Bridge of the Gard) was constructed to carry water across the Gard River to the Roman-occupied French city of Nîmes (above and page 90).

AS THE WATER FLOWS

The Latin term for "aqueduct," *aqueductus,* is from the Latin word *aquae* (of water) and *ductus* (a leading). Most of the water entering Rome came from the Anio River and its springs located in the foothills of the Apennines.

The ancients followed several rules when seeking suitable sources of water. Whenever a new fount was found, the surrounding land was dug out to create a reservoir where the water could accumulate. This area was enclosed with a wall. Since the Romans had no pumps or engines to force the water to flow down or up under pressure, as we do in our water systems, the reservoir had to be located above the channels of the aqueduct so that the water could flow down the slope and into the channel.

The Romans usually built the channels of travertine or peperino, two types of stone common to central Italy. The trough of the channel was of brick or stone and lined with a very hard cement made of lime-pounded brick or pottery and pozzolana (a volcanic rock used in making hydraulic cement, which hardens underwater). The Romans usually covered the channels to protect the flowing water from storms, exposure to the sun, and contamination by airborne objects. However, because Roman engineers believed that a totally covered channel would create problems with air pressure, they made air holes at regular intervals in the roof of the channel or in the sides when one channel was placed on top of another. To ventilate the channels that ran below ground, they constructed shafts of masonry to carry the air to the surface.

Because the water had to be transported across great distances, Roman architects had to plan for every type of terrain. Two- and three-tiered masonry arches were constructed to cross valleys. Channels built of stone blocks were used to tunnel through hills, and openings resembling channels were made in rocky cliffs.

Often lead or terra-cotta (clay) pipes were used instead of a channel or within a channel to transport the water. Each pipe was at least ten feet long. Its width depended on its use. Lead pipes were cemented together at the joints; clay pipes fit inside one another. Since a perfect setting of the joints was the key to a good system, the first water that flowed through the pipes was mixed with ashes. These ashes settled into the joint areas and further cemented them.

Because this type of pipe construction was more flexible than stone masonry, it allowed Roman engineers more latitude in planning the routes of their water systems. Water could now be carried around instead of through a hill. Also, valleys of more than one hundred fifty feet were no longer obstacles. Pipes could be placed up and down the sides and across the floor of a valley.

In Rome, the water poured into a vast reservoir called a *castellum aquarum* (shelter of waters). Usually the main castellum was a highly decorated building. Inside was one vast, cement-lined chamber with a vaulted roof supported by massive pillars. Pipes carried the water from this castellum to three smaller castella (the plural of castellum) located throughout

PREVENTIVE MAINTENANCE

A tremendous amount of care went into overseeing the aqueduct system. Before Octavius Caesar (later known as Augustus) became the ruler of the Roman world in 31 B.C., public officials known as censors maintained and regulated the waterworks. Augustus recognized the need for a special board of overseers and created the position of water commissioner. By the end of the first century A.D., this branch of the government consisted of several officials, who supervised more than four hundred fifty maintenance workers.

The construction of new pipes and major repairs were done by private contractors. To control the need for repairs, the Roman government passed a variety of regulations. One law stipulated that a strip of land fifteen feet wide on either side of an aqueduct was to be kept absolutely free and untouched, especially of plantings whose roots might damage the aqueduct.

To create a smoothly flowing water channel down the side and across the floor of a valley, an elbow-shaped piece of cement was formed with a round hole through the center. The pipe extending down the hill fit into the top opening and the valley-floor pipe into the other opening. Essential to a continuous flow of water was a gradual sloping of the channels and pipes. As a result, many aqueducts took quite a circuitous route before reaching their final destination.

Due to the effect of climatic changes on construction materials, repairs were frequently required. Here again, the Romans' superior understanding of the principles of engineering is evident. When an aqueduct was closed for repair, the water flowing in the channel had to be stopped. To prevent a water shortage, the Romans often built reservoirs at convenient points along the aqueduct's course so that if one section required some type of maintenance, only that length had to be closed.

the city. The system was so well engineered that one of the smaller castella received any excess water, which was then used in public ponds and fountains. Whenever a water shortage occurred, the public officials immediately closed this reservoir.

The flow of water was controlled by using various-sized pipes. Records were kept of the amount of water being distributed. Businesses, homeowners, and the state were all assessed for their water use. In early Rome, citizens were forbidden to divert any water from the aqueducts for private use. Only the water that escaped because of flaws in the pipes and channels could be used. Later this law was revised to allow private individuals to insert a branch pipe into the main pipe or channel to divert water into castella privata (private water shelters). A lead cistern was built within the house to collect and store the water.

THE MAGNIFICENT COLOSSEUM

> *"Quamdiu stabit Coliseus, stabit et Roma;*
>
> *Quamdiu cadit Coliseus, cadet et Roma;*
>
> *Quando cadit Roma, cadet et mundus."*
>
> "While the Colosseum stands, Rome will stand;
>
> When the Colosseum falls, Rome will fall;
>
> When Rome falls, the world will fall."
>
> The Venerable Bede (A.D. 672/73–735),
> English historian and Benedictine monk

The Venerable Bede's prophecy may still prove to be correct. Although people, in their quest for power, prosperity, and progress, have caused great damage to the Colosseum as well as to Rome, both still stand, and the world continues.

Begun during the rule of the Roman emperor Vespasian (A.D. 69–79), the Colosseum was officially dedicated the year after Vespasian's death by his son and successor, Titus.[1] Within its walls, surrounded by a dazzling display of magnificence and extravagance, the poorest citizen could share in the wealth and power of the empire. No mention of any riot or uncontrollable crowd appears in any of the works by ancient authors.

For generations, the magnificence and size of the gladiatorial combats and other games held in the Colosseum increased as each emperor attempted to outdo his predecessor. Gradually, however, as Christianity and its philosophy of the value of life

---

1. Titus died in A.D. 81, and the Colosseum was completed the following year by Domitian, Titus's brother and successor.

began to spread across the Roman world, the spectacles ceased to appeal to the masses. Early in the fifth century, an irate monk named Telemachus leaped into the arena in an attempt to snatch the weapons from two gladiators. The crazed spectators turned on the monk and stoned him to death. Soon thereafter, a law was passed forbidding gladiatorial combats. The *venationes,* fights between animals or between animals and men, were not abolished until the sixth century.

Earthquakes in 492 and 508 caused some portions of the Colosseum to fall. The collapse of half of the outer shell was probably the result of a ninth-century earthquake. Contemporary accounts note that fallen blocks of travertine and other decorations were hauled away to build palaces, bridges, and other structures. In fact, entire buildings were constructed using pieces of the Colosseum. Even the marble façade was stripped and reused, and several of the marble chairs once used by Roman senators and dignitaries stand today in Rome's churches.

The Colosseum was never completely vacated. From time to time, squatters lived there. A powerful Italian family once used it as their home and fortress. The arcades became chapels, and religious plays were performed within its walls. In the fourteenth century, bullfights were held in the arena. The destruction continued, however, as cartload after cartload of travertine blocks was hauled away. In the eighteenth century, the Colosseum became a depository for manure, which was used in the production of saltpeter (an ingredient needed to make explosives). Decades later, the Colosseum was consecrated to the memory of the Christians who had suffered martyrdom within its walls.[2]

Gradually, the willful destruction ceased, and conscientious efforts continue to be made to strengthen its walls and inner structure. Unfortunately, the future of the Colosseum is uncertain. Noise, air, and environmental pollution threaten the magnificent structure with irreparable damage.

---

2. Many scholars maintain that no Christians were martyred in the Colosseum.

THE STRUCTURE ITSELF

The Colosseum's design was daring and attested to the superb skill and artistry of its architects, artisans, and craftsmen. Wooden arenas had been the norm, erected for a particular show and then quickly leveled. It was only in 30 B.C. that the first stone amphitheater was built. Three years later, a catastrophe in the town of Fidenae, located just five miles northeast of Rome, radically changed the rules governing the construction of amphitheaters.

Thousands of people had crowded into a newly erected amphitheater in Fidenae. Suddenly, while all intently watched the gladiators fighting for their lives, they heard a great noise as the staging began to buckle. Pandemonium broke out as the boards cracked and broke. Panic followed, as the spectators fought to escape from the collapsing building. Thousands died in the catastrophe. The contractors were held responsible for their hasty and unsatisfactory work, and henceforth Roman magistrates urged the construction of only stone amphitheaters.

As a result of disasters such as the one at Fidenae and of seating problems at other amphitheaters, Roman architects constantly rethought and revised their designs. The Colosseum was their crowning achievement. Measuring 615 by 510 feet and covering an area of nearly 5 acres, it seated approximately 50,000 people (estimated by allowing approximately 23 inches of sitting space per person). The walls, rising nearly 160 feet high, were of brick, tufa limestone, and travertine, all faced with white marble.

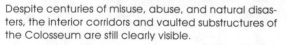
Despite centuries of misuse, abuse, and natural disasters, the interior corridors and vaulted substructures of the Colosseum are still clearly visible.

Numerous niches were adorned with statues, and the ceilings of the arches were gilded. Fountains cooled the interior. On the ground floor of this four-story structure, eighty numbered entrances provided easy and quick access to the assigned sections and seats. Seventy-six entrances were for the public; the other four, at the main axes, were for the emperor, dignitaries, and gladiators and for the removal of dead gladiators.

The substructure of this enormous building included passageways, cages for beasts, cells for gladiators, and corridors to hold props and scenery for gladiatorial shows and wild-beast hunts. The Romans always made a special effort to create authentic settings for the great array of exotic beasts and gladiators recruited from the empire's many provinces.

This reconstructed view of Imperial Rome shows how the Colosseum dwarfed its neighbors.

"THERE WILL BE AWNINGS!"

The Amphitheatrum Flavium was an engineering marvel. The architects had discussed and evaluated every need and possible emergency. Adjustments and additions were made wherever necessary. Because the Colosseum's high walls prevented any breeze from entering, the architects designed a *velarium* (awning) that extended from the perimeter walls out over the spectators. To allow light and air to enter, an elliptical or circular area above the arena was left open, leaving only the combatants exposed to the burning Mediterranean sun.

To encourage prospective spectators to attend the events, placards advertising gladiatorial contests announced *"Vela erunt!"* ("There will be awnings!"). When the Roman emperor Caligula (A.D. 37–41) attended the spectacles, which he did quite frequently, he often ordered all the spectators to remain where they were and then commanded the velarium to be drawn back. Usually the cruel Caligula waited for the hottest part of the day before giving this order.

How the awning worked is a question that archaeologists, architects, and builders have debated for centuries. Although many believe that the question will never be completely answered, some facts are clear. The fourth story of the Colosseum was a simple wall divided into sections by eighty pilasters.[1] A small window in every other section allowed daylight to enter. On the inside of the wall was a covered portico. Here the seats were wooden, in contrast to the rest of the structure, which was built mostly of travertine, a decorative limestone quarried near Tivoli, a town northeast of Rome. (A specially cut road, six feet wide, was used for transporting these blocks to Rome.)

Between the pilasters were three projecting brackets and sockets to support the two hundred forty masts that held the awning. A visitor today can see, from street level, the corresponding holes in the cornice (projection) above, through which the masts were set for support and stability. Stone slabs at ground level may have been markers to help with crowd control, but many scholars believe that they also helped with the great number of ropes needed to work the awning. It is thought that a corps of specially trained sailors worked this complex rigging and the awning. But how it was unfurled, how many sections it had, and what held it straight and kept it from collapsing are unanswered questions.

---

1. A pilaster is a rectangular support that is treated architecturally as a column but is not freestanding.

WHAT'S IN A NAME?

The structure known to us today as the Colosseum was an *amphitheatrum* (amphitheater) to the Romans. A combination of the Greek terms *amphi* (on both sides) and *theatron* (an area where something is seen or viewed), an amphitheater is a place where a public spectacle can be seen by those seated on both sides of an arena. Hence, an amphitheater resembles two theaters placed back to back. Because the one in Rome was built and dedicated by emperors whose family name was Flavius, it was called the Amphitheatrum Flavium[1] (Flavian Amphitheater) in their honor.

Even after the amphitheater ceased to be used for public spectacles, visitors continued to marvel at its size and beauty. Many began referring to it as a *colossos,* from the Greek term *kolossos,* meaning "something gigantic." Sometime during the Middle Ages (A.D. 400–1400), the Amphitheatrum Flavium became the Colosseum.

---

1. When used as an adjective to modify the neuter noun *amphitheatrum,* Flavius becomes Flavium.

MOCK NAVAL BATTLES

The site of the Colosseum was uniquely suited to its purpose. It had once housed the swimming pool of the Roman emperor Nero (A.D. 54–68). Since Nero's reign had been marked by many cruel incidents, all traces of the emperor were eliminated after his assassination.

Vespasian's architects quickly claimed the pool site because it was the perfect substructure for the magnificent amphitheater the emperor had commissioned. After the water was drained, the cavern was carefully sectioned off, and specially fit wooden boards were placed on the walls of the substructure. Sand and whatever props or scenery were required for a show were then placed on the boards.

The architects of this grand amphitheater designed the arena and the area below so that it could be flooded with water to allow warships to battle each other.[1] Scholars still do not agree on the exact method the Romans used to convert the Colosseum into a lake, but several ancient authors mention the *naumachiae* (naval battles) they witnessed in the Amphitheatrum Flavium.

What a sight it must have been! Imagine the field of one of today's stadia flooded, two naval ships floating a short distance apart, a bugle sounding, and the battle beginning. Even with our advanced technology, it is difficult to conceive of such a contest.

---

1. Scholars believe that after the elaborate subterranean system of cages and compartments was completed, flooding the area was no longer possible, and mock naval battles were held elsewhere.

HADRIAN'S MAUSOLEUM

In A.D. 135, the eighteenth year of his rule, the Roman emperor Publius Aelius Hadrianus initiated the construction of his mausoleum. As the site lay on the banks of the Tiber River, he also commissioned his architects to build a bridge, the Aelian Bridge, that would lead directly to the mausoleum. Hadrian died in 138, one year prior to its completion. Hadrian's successor, Antoninus Pius (138–161), had Hadrian's remains transferred to the grand burial chamber in the mausoleum, which became the official resting place of all succeeding emperors until the third century.[1]

The general design of the mausoleum consisted of an immense circular drum about two hundred thirty feet in diameter set on a square base. Each side of the base measured approximately three hundred thirty feet. To soften the effect of such a towering solid mass, a series of attached columns (pilasters) and colonnades graced the structure. The columns were of richly colored imported marble and porphyry (a type of rock consisting of feldspar crystals embedded in a dark red or purple groundmass). In addition, the entire façade was covered with marble, mostly white.

On top of each corner of the base was a group of equestrian statues. Between the columns and on the circular drum were numerous other statues. Rising above all this was a cone-shaped marble dome surrounded by cypress trees and crowned either with a gigantic sculpture of Hadrian or a majestic bronze figure of the sun god Apollo in his *quadriga* (an ancient chariot drawn by four horses).

The inner core, much of which still exists today, was constructed of large blocks of peperino and travertine. These blocks surrounded an inner mass of concrete, where the central burial chamber and the passages leading to it were located. All the surfaces were covered with rich Oriental marble and paved with mosaics. To allow light to enter, vertical shafts reached from the main floor to the basement.

---

1. Sources differ as to who was the last emperor buried in the mausoleum.

Built to serve as a reminder of Hadrian's and Rome's greatness, this structure remained a revered monument for approximately two hundred years. As Rome's power diminished, invading troops became more daring. But Rome would not fall without a struggle. The emperor Aurelian (270–275) built a wall around the city and connected Hadrian's mausoleum to it. Thus, it was a Roman emperor, not a foreigner, who first defaced the grand edifice.

Decades later, in August of 410, Alaric and his Visigoths[2] invaded Rome, plundering it mercilessly. Fortunately, the monument was left untouched, but the treasured urns within the mausoleum were broken, and the ashes of the dead emperors mixed with those of the plundered city.

Visitors from around the world cross the Tiber River on Hadrian's Aelian Bridge to admire the enormous structure he constructed to house his remains.

FROM TOMB TO FORTRESS

In A.D. 488, Theodoric the Great, king of the Ostrogoths, invaded Italy. Four years later, his conquest complete, he named himself king of Italy. Theodoric restored Rome's walls and fortified Hadrian's mausoleum. Yet his efforts were in vain. After his death, invaders from the north again descended on Rome.

Recognizing that the mausoleum was stronger

---

2. The Goths were a Germanic people whose military forces harassed the Roman Empire for centuries. The Ostrogoths were the eastern Goths, who conquered and settled the lands from Italy to Constantinople. The Visigoths were the western Goths, who conquered and settled the lands from France to Spain and Portugal.

Through the centuries, Romans have protected and preserved the statue of the angel sheathing its sword atop the huge stone drum that was once Hadrian's mausoleum. Weathered or damaged statues are always replaced.

than any existing fortress or citadel, Rome's inhabitants fled to it for refuge. Their efforts to defeat the attacking Goths were so desperate that they pulled down the magnificent statues, snapped and hammered them into large pieces, and hurled the heavy fragments onto the heads of the enemy. The strategy worked, and the invaders retreated, never to return. Shorn now of its beauty, the mausoleum assumed its new role as a fortress and citadel of Rome.

At the end of the sixth century, a deadly plague swept through the city. In desperation, Pope Gregory the Great[1] took a revered picture of Mary, the mother of Jesus Christ, and paraded it through the streets of the city. As he approached the Aelian Bridge, Gregory looked toward the mausoleum. Awestruck, he turned away and looked again. There, above the tower's summit, he saw a mighty angel sheathing a bloody sword. Believing that this omen meant that the great plague was over, Pope Gregory rejoiced and sought an appropriate way to commemorate this event. He renamed the mausoleum Castel Sant'Angelo (Castle of the Blessed Angel) and commissioned the figure of an angel sheathing a sword to be placed on the summit.

During the Middle Ages, the mausoleum became the center of much intrigue and bloodshed. Owing to the thickness and strength of the concrete mass, it had become an impregnable fortress. Dungeons, miserable prison cells, and vats were hollowed out of the interior. These vats were used to hold water and to boil oil for pouring on the heads of attackers. Enormous storerooms were created to hold provisions that could feed the garrison and all the inhabitants during a siege.

1. The pope, the chief pontiff and representative of the Catholic Church, is now headquartered in Rome.

As the Catholic Church became more prominent and powerful, the mausoleum became the stage for many religious struggles. A passageway was built linking the Vatican, the pope's headquarters, with the mausoleum to allow the pope to escape to the mighty fortress whenever his life was in danger.

As a result of this constant activity within Hadrian's mausoleum, battlements and other prerequisites for a well-equipped garrison were constantly being installed. Luxurious staterooms were added during the sixteenth century to accommodate visiting heads of state, church officials, and other nobles.

In 1752, a colossal bronze angel, made by the Dutch sculptor Pietro van Vershaffelt, was added to the summit. This angel still stands atop the mausoleum. An earlier marble statue by Raffaello da Montelupo stands in the courtyard. (Many statues have stood on the summit. One was stolen, and others were destroyed during numerous battles around the edifice.)

The nineteenth century witnessed a renewed respect for the ancient resting place of Rome's emperors. Church and state no longer used the mausoleum as a battleground, and on September 29, 1870, the pope and the papal garrison evacuated the mausoleum. Shortly thereafter, the flag of Italy fluttered beside the figure of the angel.

Today Hadrian's tomb, more widely known as the Castel Sant'Angelo, is a museum open to the public. Although it is difficult to imagine how this grand edifice looked in the past, the imposing remains and the size and strength of the inner core allow visitors to imagine the voices of the people who steered the course of history for so many generations.

CONSTRUCT A ROMAN ROAD

The key to the success of the Roman road system was its thick substructure composed of various materials. The Romans realized that this combination aided drainage and provided flexibility and give to their roads. The standard paved road consisted of several layers.

Native earth: First the ground was leveled and pounded so that it would be very firm. Should the ground remain soft, wooden pieces were wedged into the earth to tighten the area involved.

Statumen: A thick layer (about eight inches) of stones of a size that would fit in the hand.

Rudus: A layer of rubble or concrete about three inches thick composed of broken stones and lime.

Nucleus: A bedding of fine cement made of pounded potsherds (pieces of broken pottery) and lime.

Dorsum: The "crown" of the road was paved with large polygonal blocks of lava or rectangular blocks of hard stone. It was constructed in such a way that the middle section was higher than the sides, allowing rain and water to run off. Sometimes the stones were cut to a point at the bottom so as to grasp the next layer better. Each stone was trimmed so that all fit closely together, thereby ensuring the durability of the road.

Crepido, margo, or **semita:** A raised footway or sidewalk on either side of the road.

Umbones and **gomphi:** Umbones (edge stones) were used to strengthen and support the walkway. Gomphi (curbstones) of greater size and height were placed at intervals in the line of umbones. These gomphi were found in and near cities.

Another block over here! Hop to it!

CAVETE VIAM MUNIUNT

DORSUM

NUCLEUS

RUDUS

STATUMEN

NATIVE EARTH

You Need

scissors
2 sheets of plain white paper
shoe box bottom or similar rectangular box
glue
ruler
pen or felt-tip marker
plastic wrap
Scotch tape or masking tape
dirt (enough to make a 1/2-inch layer in the box)
round toothpicks
small stones, each no larger than a pea (enough to make a 1 1/2-inch layer in the box)
twigs broken into pieces (enough to make a 1-inch layer in the box)
popcorn kernels (enough to make a 1/2-inch layer in the box)
small, flat stones or small rectangular wooden blocks, some thicker than others

1. Refer regularly to the list of layers used by Roman road engineers.
2. Cut the white paper to cover the sides of the box. Glue it in place.
3. Place the ruler vertically at each corner of the box. Mark each layer: 1/2 inch, 1 1/2 inches, 1 inch, 1/2 inch. Connect the marks by drawing a line across each side of the box.
4. Using the pen or marker, write the name (Native Earth, Statumen, Rudus, Nucleus, Dorsum) for each layer.
5. With a scissors, cut off one of the narrow ends of the shoe box.
6. Take a piece of plastic wrap, fold it in half, and place it across the open end of the box. Make sure the top of the box and the folded edge of the wrap are even. Pull the other edges of the plastic wrap so that it fits tightly. Tape the three edges to the box.
7. Cover the box bottom with 1/2 inch of dirt. Press it down firmly. Insert pieces of toothpicks where the dirt seems a little loose.
8. Place a 1 1/2-inch layer of small stones on top of the dirt. Make sure they fit snugly together.
9. Place a 1-inch layer of small broken twigs on the stones.
10. Place a 1/2-inch layer of popcorn kernels on the twigs.
11. Place the thickest flat stones (or wooden blocks) on top of the corn kernels along the middle section. Fill in the side areas with the remaining flat stones (or wooden blocks).

this will make the box nice and pretty!

I'll measure the lines!

STATUMEN NATIVE EARTH

I'll write the names of the layers!

Now you have a see-through window!

snip snip

carefully put each layer in the box!

popcorn kernels
twigs
small stones
Dirt

Finish up top with flat stones or wooden blocks!

start down here with dirt!

Wow! No potholes!

DORSUM NUCLEUS RUDUS STATUMEN NATIVE EARTH

– illustrated by Annette Cate

A WET SCRAMBLE

Unscramble the ten words below to determine the answers to the clues. Then place the numbered letters on the corresponding blank lines to discover what the Romans used to collect household water. The answers can be found in the articles on aqueducts, pages 90–93, and on page 151.

1. These were two of Rome's earliest aqueducts.
acamipirapa   _ _ _ _ _ _ _ _ _ _ _
                9   13   8

2. Much of Rome's water came from these hills.
snainepen   _ _ _ _ _ _ _ _ _
                      11

3. He was the first Roman emperor to appoint a water commissioner.
satusugu   _ _ _ _ _ _ _ _
                  4

4. Whenever a new fount was found, Roman engineers created one of these to hold the water.
vesirorer   _ _ _ _ _ _ _ _ _
                  5

5. An aqueduct's channels were often made of this.
ritnatvere   _ _ _ _ _ _ _ _ _ _
                   12

6. In Rome, the aqueducts poured water into this enormous reservoir.
quumaclraumastle   _ _ _ _ _ _ _ _ _ _ _ _ _ _ _
                    1   6   15

7. As water commissioner, he oversaw Rome's aqueducts.
ritunsofn   _ _ _ _ _ _ _ _
                      3

8. This type of volcanic rock was used to make a type of cement that hardened underwater.
zoanzalpo   _ _ _ _ _ _ _ _ _
                  7

9. Romans used lead or this substance to make their pipes.
tactetaror   _ _ _ _ _ _ _ _ _ _ _
                  2   14

10. This river in Rome did not produce enough water to meet the city's needs.
betri   _ _ _ _ _
              10

Romans used these to collect household water:

_ _ _ _ _ _ _ _ _ _ _ _ _ _ _
1 2 3 4 5 6 7 8 9 10 11 12 13 14 15

A COLOSSAL PUZZLE

Use the clues to fill in the blanks. The letters in the boxes will spell the name of the emperor responsible for constructing the Colosseum. The answers can be found in the articles on the Colosseum, pages 94–99, and on page 151.

1. This protected the Colosseum's spectators from the sun.
2. Fights between animals or animals and men.
3. More than two hundred of these were believed to hold the awning over the Colosseum.
4. In later centuries, the Colosseum's arcades were turned into these.
5. Mock naval battles held in the Colosseum.

6. The word "colosseum" is derived from this Greek term meaning "something gigantic."
7. This is a modern threat to the Colosseum.
8. This was the Colosseum's original name in English.
9. Type of stone blocks used to construct the Colosseum.

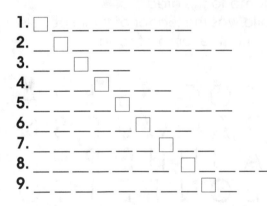

1. ☐ _ _ _ _ _ _ _
2. _ ☐ _ _ _ _ _ _ _ _
3. _ _ ☐ _ _
4. _ _ _ ☐ _ _ _
5. _ _ _ _ ☐ _ _ _ _ _
6. _ _ _ _ _ ☐ _ _
7. _ _ _ _ _ _ ☐ _ _
8. _ _ _ _ _ _ _ ☐ _ _ _ _ _ _ _ _ _
9. _ _ _ _ _ _ _ ☐ _

A WORDY FORTRESS

Use the clues to find the twenty-two words hidden in the maze. The answers can be found in the articles on Hadrian's Mausoleum, pages 100–103, and on page 151. Hint: To help you on your way, the name used today for Hadrian's tomb has been highlighted.

This bridge leads to Hadrian's tomb

What Pope Gregory saw atop the tomb

Hadrian's successor

Roman sun god

Emperor who connected the tomb to Rome's walls

The dome was surrounded by these trees

The general shape of Hadrian's tomb

During the Middle Ages, these were hollowed out of the tomb

Rome is located here

Many columns were made of this

Another name for a tomb

The inner core of the tomb is paved with these

Hadrian's tomb today

They invaded Italy

The inner core is made of blocks of these two materials

This type of column was used on Hadrian's tomb

He fortified the mausoleum

Hadrian's tomb is on the bank of this river

A later passageway connected the tomb to this area

Alaric was the leader of these people

Color of the tomb's façade

```
M C T P I L P S S H T O G I S I V A
A U S T E R S E C Y P A M W U R S N
C A S E D E L I P N A U N H D R H T
I U N E R G E E A E E O N I E I T O
R V V P U A T I N L R D C T A T O N
O M Y A M M L N O I U I S E L A G I
D C A S T E L S A N T A N G E L O N
O T P R A I U H G I L R N O E Y R U
E O O D B A C E O I L R E G I C T S
H O L S M L O A P T R E O V E G S P
T O L T H N E S N G O T R T A L O I
I B O P S E M O S A I C S U T R R U
W H I M A T I B E R A P I G A E T S
```

COMPANION

Topics for Comparison

1. Compare and contrast Rome's international road system with the U.S. interstate highway system. Compare also the use of signs (milestones for the Romans). Compare the periods in the histories of both nations that prompted the introduction of such systems.

2. Compare the construction of modern roads with the methods used to build Roman roads.

3. Compare U.S. reservoirs and water systems with those built by the Romans. Can sections be shut off in the United States as they were in ancient Rome?

4. Compare and contrast Roman arenas such as the Colosseum with twentieth-century sports stadia in size, construction, crowd control, exits, food concessions, covered domes, use of a variety of turfs, and boxes for VIPs.

5. Compare the Romans' use of Hadrian's mausoleum as a "cemetery" for emperors with Arlington National Cemetery in Virginia and its use today as a cemetery for outstanding leaders.

Suggestions for Writing Assignments

1. Today's laws forbid the use of lead in household paints because of the detrimental effects lead can have if consumed. Research the use of lead in ancient Rome. Could lead have entered the Romans' systems and contributed to the decline of Rome and the weaknesses exhibited by many of the later emperors?

2. Research the rule of Hadrian. How did he affect Rome? The mausoleum was not Hadrian's only grand construction project. Research his villa and the Pantheon. How do the structures he commissioned still affect Rome?

3. Explain how the Roman road system reflects Rome's quest for power.

4. Find the oldest existing structure in your community. Research the various purposes the structure has served. List them chronologically and tell why each change was made. If the use of the structure has remained the same, discuss why you think this is so.

5. No matter what the century or country, people love spectacles. In today's world, what spectacles have replaced the events that took place in ancient times in the Colosseum?

6. Of the four structures discussed in this chapter, list them in order of their importance to the growth and well-being of Rome (lowest first). Explain your reasoning.

Further Activities

1. Make a time line of the buildings discussed in this chapter. For each, include the date of construction, the dates of the emperor(s) under whom it was built, the dedication date (if different from the date of completion), the date it ceased to be used for its original purpose, and the date when it assumed its present role (if any).

2. Go to the library and ask for a recording of Respighi's *The Pines of Rome.* Listen to the movement "Pines of the Appian Way." Write down your thoughts about the composer's motives and how you think the piece reflects them.

3. Research the location of aqueducts that were built by the Romans and are still standing today.

4. The Colosseum was built on the foundation of Nero's swimming pool. This reuse of parts of older structures is common today. Look around your city or town. Are there any buildings that were built on the foundations of other structures?

5. Historians still do not know exactly how the Romans flooded their amphitheaters for the *naumachiae.* Develop your own theory. Keep in mind how the Roman aqueduct system worked and incorporate it into your theory.

Topics for Debate

1. The Romans spent too much time and effort building and maintaining the Colosseum, a building dedicated to cruelty and suffering.

2. The sports stadia of today have replaced the Roman amphitheaters.

"Everything is deemed miraculous when it is first discovered, just as so much is judged impossible before it actually occurs."

Pliny the Elder, first-century A.D. Roman historian and naturalist

GREEK CREATIVITY

CHAPTER

The inventors are presented in chronological order.

ARCHIMEDES

Archimedes was born around 287 B.C. in Syracuse, Sicily, an island in the Mediterranean Sea just west of southern Italy. Of the few facts known about his life, one is certain: He spent a considerable amount of time studying in Egypt in the city of Alexandria, the center of scientific learning in the ancient world.

Archimedes devised several principles and methods that form the basis for mathematics. Among these are (1) the formula for finding the volume of a cylinder, (2) the formula for measuring circles and ellipses, (3) a system to enumerate numbers as large as might be desired, (4) the ratio of a cylinder to a circle within it, (5) the method of calculating π (π is the Greek letter pi, which represents the ratio of the circumference of a circle to its diameter), and (6) the basic principles of integral calculus. Today, as the fields of science, mathematics, and technology move into the twenty-first century, the discoveries and theories advanced by Archimedes still stand, unchanged and undisputed.

THE WATER SCREW

The land bordering Egypt's Nile River was always extremely fertile because the Nile overflowed its banks every year[1] and its waters acted as fertilizer. Throughout the rest of Egypt, rain fell infrequently and farmers used buckets to haul water from the river to their fields. Archimedes's invention of the water screw[2] was revolutionary. Farmers throughout Egypt readily adopted it.

To construct his water screw, Archimedes used a long, thick screw with good-size threads (making his invention similar in appearance to a huge corkscrew). He attached a handle to the top of the screw

1. Since the completion of the Aswan High Dam in 1970, the annual flooding of the Nile has been controlled mechanically.

2. Some sources state that a type of water screw predated that of Archimedes.

and then encased the screw in a cylinder. The open-ended bottom section of the cylinder with the screw inside was put in the water, while the top section rested on the land. To set the screw in operation, a worker turned the handle. The water entered the cylinder and "climbed" along the threads of the screw before pouring out the top of the cylinder. To catch the water, farmers placed buckets underneath the top or used pipes or channels to carry the water to their fields.

In some areas of Egypt today, farmers still use Archimedes's screw to irrigate their fields. Sailors use the screw to empty bilge water. Propellers work on basically the same principle as the water screw, because they move machines forward by spinning the air or water behind. In Holland, Archimedes's invention is used in reverse—to move water from the land back into the canals.

THE LEVER AND FULCRUM

Another of Archimedes's inventions resulted from his boast "If I had another earth on which to place my feet, I could move this earth." Archimedes sincerely believed that if he had the proper leverage and force, he could move the world. His friends, however, did not believe it.

Since no other earth existed for Archimedes to prove his theory, he offered to move any object the ruler of Syracuse, Hieron II, might choose. Hieron took up the challenge and chose a huge ship he had just built. The day was set. Archimedes prepared his mechanical devices: pulleys and ropes, all based on the principle of the lever and fulcrum (the point or support on which a lever turns). Many came to witness the "mad" scientist's defeat. Archimedes was confident and, with a minimum of effort, moved the ship.

Today the principle of the lever and fulcrum forms the basis for countless tools and pieces of equipment. Sticks, screwdrivers, oars, and pulleys are all levers.

GOLD VERSUS SILVER

Another of Archimedes's discoveries involved a gold crown that Hieron II had ordered. After the goldsmith presented Hieron with the crown, Hieron thought it weighed less than it should have and that the goldsmith had not used pure gold but a mixture of gold and silver. The problem was how to prove it.

Hieron summoned Archimedes. Before long, Archimedes was so involved in finding a solution that he neglected his own bodily needs. His slaves were accustomed to this behavior and were constantly after him to eat, drink, and wash. Perhaps this was fortunate, for one day, as he stepped into a tub brimming with water, he noticed water spilling out. Without stopping to clothe himself, he ran out into the street shouting, *"Eureka! Eureka!"* ("I have found it! I have found it!").

What Archimedes had discovered was the basic principle of hydrostatics, the science that deals with the laws of nature governing liquids at rest. Archimedes took a lump of gold equal to the amount of gold that Hieron had ordered for the crown. If the lump and the crown each displaced the same amount of water, Archimedes reasoned, the two were identical in weight. Archimedes placed the lump of gold in a container filled with water. He carefully measured the water that ran out as the lump entered. Then he placed the crown in an identical container and measured the water that flowed out. The crown displaced less water than the lump. The goldsmith had cheated.

As a result of this experiment, Archimedes and others had a specific method to differentiate one substance from another. Hieron's crown also helped Archimedes discover the principles of buoyancy and specific gravity. Not until the 1800s and the experiments of the French scientist Blaise Pascal were any new laws added to hydraulics.

CTESIBIUS

Facts about Ctesibius's life are few. The son of a barber, he was born during the third century B.C. in the Egyptian city of Alexandria. At an early age, he became known for his mechanical ability and ingenuity. Which inventions are his and what modifications he made to other inventions may never be known for certain because none of his works has survived. However, both the water organ and the water clock are commonly attributed to him.

THE WATER ORGAN

The diagram included here is a modern reconstruction of Ctesibius's water organ. To create and maintain a steady flow of air, a person pressed the lever arm (H). This action moved the piston (B) upward in the cylinder (A), which in turn forced the air in the cylinder to pass through the valve (C) and into a globe. If the piston sank down by its own weight, air was drawn back into the cylinder and again forced into the globe (D). The air that accumulated in the globe pressed down on the water surrounding it, causing the water level to rise. The pressure of this water made the air in the globe and the box (E) rush through the organ pipe (G). When a musician struck a key (F), the stopper piece below the organ pipe was pushed back until a passageway for air was created from the globe to the organ pipe—producing a sound. The length and width of the individual pipes determined the type of sound.

THE WATER CLOCK

The ancients commonly used sundials, but this timepiece had many drawbacks. It required sun, gave only the approximate time, and required special positioning in respect to the longitude and latitude of each location.

Water clocks date back to at least 1500 B.C. The ancients used the water clock in the courtroom to limit the time a lawyer could speak. Exactly how the water clock worked is not certain. Hermann Diels,

HEY! YOUR WATER'S UP!

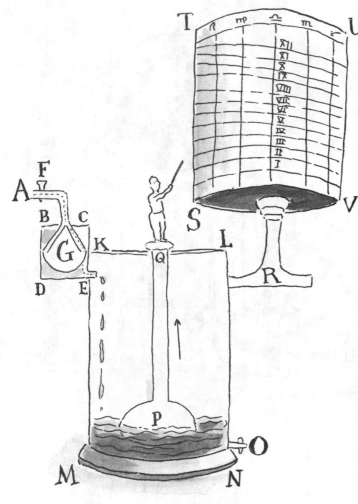

an early twentieth-century German scientist, is credited with the best reproduction and explanation of how the water clock developed or enhanced by Ctesibius might have functioned.

Water flowed through a pipe (A) into a holding vessel (G). From this holding vessel, the water slowly dripped via the small opening (E) into a cylinder (KLMN). The mechanism was advanced enough to enable users to control the rate of flow and make it uniform. Therefore, the amount of water collecting in the vessel provided a fairly accurate measure of time. To indicate the amount of time that had passed, a float (P) was attached by a rod to a stand (Q) on which stood a figure with a pointer in his hands. Attached to cylinder KLMN was the base (R) of another cylinder (TUSV).

Around the upper rim of cylinder TUSV are the twelve signs of the zodiac. Along the side of the cylinder is a graduated scale. The ancients divided daytime into twelve hours and nighttime into twelve hours. Hence, the length of the hour varied according to the season—that is, shorter daytime hours and longer nighttime hours in winter and vice versa in summer. The graduated scale took all this into account. As the water rose in cylinder KLMN, the pointer indicated the hour on cylinder TUSV. When the float had risen to the top, the day was done. The hole at the bottom of cylinder KLMN (O) was then unplugged to allow the water to exit, and the process began again.

HERO

In the first century A.D., a mathematician and inventor named Hero lived in the Egyptian city of Alexandria. He wrote about his own inventions and often described other machines and principles he had seen or heard about. His writings have provided valuable historical information in the fields of mathematics and applied mechanics.

Hero spent most of his time on inventions that were fanciful and entertaining, not laborsaving devices, because the society in which he lived was based on abundant slave labor. Hero used a pump to sound a toy trumpet and toothed wheels to move puppets. He constructed a machine that dispensed holy water when a coin was deposited in a slot. He even designed a mechanism that opened temple doors when a fire was lit on the altar. Several of the inventions attributed to Hero are described here in Hero's own words.

THE STEAM ENGINE

Place a cauldron on a stand over a hearth. Fill the cauldron with water and light a fire underneath. Cover the cauldron and bring the water to a boil. Attach a tube to the cover so that it extends into the cauldron and also above the lid. Bend the top part of the tube at a right angle and connect it with an airtight joint to a hollow ball. On the opposite side of the ball, place another tube with a pivot between it and the ball. Have its base rest on the lid. In addition, attach to the ball two tubes, bent at right angles, perpendicular to the tubes extending up from the lid, and diametrically opposite one another on the ball. Point the ends in opposite directions.

117

"As the water boils, steam enters the ball through the tube, then pours out through the openings in the bent tubes. When the steam hits the lid, it causes the ball to revolve."

THE WHISTLING BIRD

Attach a figure of a bird to the tip of a pipe or tube (D) that juts out from a container. Place a toothed wheel halfway up the pipe. Run a second pipe through the container and perpendicular to the 'bird's' pipe. Its inner end is pointed to revolve on a base. A toothed wheel on it connects with the first toothed wheel. Place a small container with water at the end of the pipe extending out from the container. In the small container, place a smaller hollow container with no bottom (V) and with a pipe leading out from its side. Attach a rope from this container to the horizontal pipe.

"To make the bird rotate, turn the wheel outside the container. This action also will cause V to rise.

"To create a whistling noise, take your hand from the wheel. The rope will unwind, and will fall back into the larger container and into the water. This action will force the air in the hollow container out through the pipe, causing a whistling sound."

THE ODOMETER

Along the main roads of the Roman Empire, blocks of granite and stone marked the distance a traveler had gone and listed the distance still to go to reach a particular destination. Hero provides us with a detailed description of his invention for measuring distances:

"Five pairs of toothed elements are set at right angles to each other. Some are wheels, and others are tubes with a circular ridge jutting out. The top pair is attached to a circle marked with figures to record the distance traveled. The whole mechanism is set in motion when the pin attached to the axle of the wheel of the traveling vehicle to which the device is attached catches in the radial pegs of the bottom wheel."

ARCHIMEDES AND THE SIEGE OF SYRACUSE[1]

Characters

King Hieron[2]—*king of Syracuse*
Prince Gelon—*son of Hieron*
Archimedes—*great mathematician and inventor*
Prince Hieronymos—*grandson of Hieron and son of Gelon*
Hippokrates—*traitor who seized control of Syracuse*
Marcellus—*Roman commander*
Roman lieutenant
Roman engineer
Roman soldier

Introduction

Syracuse, a peaceful and thriving city on the island of Sicily, a Greek colony off the southern coast of Italy, was the home of the famous mathematician and inventor Archimedes. Under the reign of King Hieron II, Syracuse found itself affected by a fierce conflict involving Rome and Carthage, a powerful city-state on the north coast of Africa.

The Romans and the Carthaginians were vying for control of the Mediterranean Sea. Carthage already had colonies in Spain and claimed all of the western Mediterranean and most of Sicily except for Syracuse. Rome's armies had been capturing the Greek city-states in Italy. It was reasonable to expect

---

1. This play is a revised edition of an original play by Charles F. Baker that appeared in the September 1989 issue of *CLASSICAL CALLIOPE.*
2. Some sources spell Hieron's name Hiero.

– illustrated by Annette Cate

that Syracuse, because of its location, would be caught in a war between the rapidly growing powers.

Act I

It is the year 220 B.C. Syracuse has an alliance with Rome, but King Hieron is wondering how long it will last. Carthage has a great fleet of ships, and the Romans are spread out all over the area and cannot be relied on for protection. King Hieron needs a plan to defend his vulnerable city and turns to his long-time friend and kinsman Archimedes for advice and help.

Scene 1

The royal palace of King Hieron. The king and his son, Prince Gelon, have received news that the Romans are angry with the Carthaginians because they cannot trade in Sicily. Carthage has recently gained control of the Strait of Messina, which separates Sicily and Italy. Hieron has just sent for Archimedes.

KING HIERON: My son, I fear for the safety of our city. Rome will not tolerate the aggressive actions of Carthage, and there will be a war.

PRINCE GELON: I agree. This is a dangerous situation. Rome will be cut off from its own ports in eastern Italy. The Romans cannot even sail around Sicily because Carthage also controls the western Mediterranean. All-out war is inevitable, and we will be caught in the middle.

KING HIERON: We must prepare to defend ourselves, even though we have an alliance with Rome. They could not possibly come to our rescue against the Carthaginians. They are already fighting in many different areas and cannot spare soldiers or ships to protect our city.

PRINCE GELON: I would not trust the Romans to continue to be our allies. They are an ambitious people, and I am sure they will want to add our prosperous city to their growing empire.

KING HIERON: I think you are right. That is why I want to build up our defenses. It is my hope that I will leave a strong, independent city for you and my grandson, Prince Hieronymos, to inherit. I have sent for Archimedes so that we can discuss this serious situation with him. I value his advice.

PRINCE GELON: I also have great respect for Archimedes, but how can he help defend our city? He is only a mathematician, not a soldier.

(Archimedes enters the royal chamber and hears Prince Gelon's statement.)

ARCHIMEDES: You are right, Your Royal Highness. Since I returned to Syracuse from Egypt many years ago, I have dedicated my life entirely to mathematical research.

KING HIERON: You know as well as I do, my friend, that you have become famous for your clever mechanical inventions.

ARCHIMEDES: They are only the diversions of geometry at play, and I attach no importance to them. I regard the business of mechanics as vulgar and despicable.

KING HIERON: Syracuse is in danger of becoming involved in the war between Rome and Carthage.

ARCHIMEDES: So I have heard.

KING HIERON: Having been at peace for so many years, we have not bothered to maintain our defenses. We forgot that our city was taken by siege years ago. I do not want that to happen again. Archimedes, I implore you to use your scientific knowledge to prepare for me offensive and defensive engines that can be used in every kind of siege warfare.

121

ARCHIMEDES: I do not like the idea of using science to destroy people.

KING HIERON: Why can you not use some of your scientific knowledge to defend the city that has sheltered you and given you the freedom to do your mathematical research for so many years? I should think that you would be anxious to prove that science can provide a better means to defend Syracuse than an army can.

ARCHIMEDES: You have won. I will begin at once to devise plans for all sorts of engines to use against any besiegers.

KING HIERON: We will all be grateful for your expertise.

Scene 2
Several months later. King Hieron, Prince Gelon, Prince Hieronymos, and Archimedes are standing on the battlements of Syracuse inspecting the newly built war machines designed by the famous mathematician. Once Archimedes had set his mind to this project, he had drawn plan after plan, and each machine had been constructed by the king's workmen.

KING HIERON: I am very pleased by your fast and productive work, Archimedes. I knew we could rely on you to strengthen our city with your clever inventions.

ARCHIMEDES: Thank you, Your Majesty. I used all the knowledge about mechanics that I have gained over the years.

PRINCE GELON: Would you describe the functions of some of these war machines to us? My son, Hieronymos, and I are curious as to their use. They all look so ingeniously made.

ARCHIMEDES: I would be happy to, Your Royal

Highness. *(pointing to the various machines)* Those are catapults, which can fling heavy stones at long or short ranges. Over there are machines that can discharge showers of missiles through holes made in the walls.

PRINCE HIERONYMOS: Why are those poles jutting out beyond the walls?

ARCHIMEDES: Some of them are to be used to drop heavy stones or pieces of lead on enemy ships.

PRINCE GELON: What are those objects hanging from poles that look like beaks on enemy ships?

ARCHIMEDES: They are iron claws that will be lowered to grapple the prows of ships, lifting them into the air and swinging them until the sailors fall out, then dropping the vessels onto the rocks, where they will be smashed.

PRINCE HIERONYMOS: What are all those mirrors for?

ARCHIMEDES: I intend to use them to direct the sun's rays at the attacking ships, blinding the sailors so that they become confused and cannot fight back. They can be effective only if the sun is shining intensely, of course.

KING HIERON: Our city should be safe from any attack by our enemies. Until we are besieged, I command that these machines be stored away but kept in perfect working condition. The ropes must never become frayed, any rotted wood is to be replaced, and none of the metal can be allowed to corrode in the salt air. I also command that we always have men trained to operate the machines, even if it is years before we need to use them. Let

123

us return to the palace. Knowing that my city is well protected, I can now sleep in peace.

Act II

It is about 212 B.C. King Hieron died in 215 B.C.; his son, Prince Gelon, died a short time later. His grandson, Hieronymos, then became king of Syracuse.

Hieronymos did not stay king for long. He was murdered by a treacherous man named Hippokrates, who had been bribed by Carthage to kill the king. When Hippokrates took control of Syracuse, one of the first things he did was to break the city's alliance with Rome. He then made a new alliance with his friends in Carthage.

Rome was very angry at losing such a valuable ally and immediately declared war on Syracuse. Marcellus, a famous Roman general and a personal enemy of Hippokrates's, was sent with a large fleet and an army to seize Syracuse from the Carthaginians. He was determined to gain control of the Strait of Messina so that Roman ships could finally use it safely.

Scene 1

The battlements of Syracuse. A large Roman fleet is approaching the city, and the frightened people are pleading with Hippokrates to protect them. He has called on Archimedes to ready his war machines. The

124

mathematician does not like the traitor who now rules his city, but Archimedes must think of protecting his fellow citizens.

HIPPOKRATES: Archimedes, I beg you to use your war machines to repel the Roman besiegers. Their army surrounds us on land, and their fleet of sixty ships is about to attack us by sea.

ARCHIMEDES: Where are your friends from Carthage?

HIPPOKRATES: We cannot wait for their help. We must stop the Romans now before it is too late.

ARCHIMEDES: The machines have been kept in excellent condition since they were first built, and the men trained to operate them are ready.

HIPPOKRATES: What is that harp-shaped contraption built on a platform on those Roman ships? It looks frightening.

ARCHIMEDES: That is called a *sambuca,* after the musical instrument it resembles. It carries a broad scaling ladder that, when pulled up, makes it possible to scale walls.

HIPPOKRATES: Swarms of Roman soldiers will be pouring into our city if we do not destroy the sambuca first.

ARCHIMEDES: Do not worry. The cranes I have constructed on the walls will drop large stones on

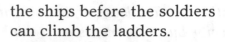

the ships before the soldiers can climb the ladders.

HIPPOKRATES: How shall we stop the land forces that are approaching?

ARCHIMEDES: I have created engines that will shoot all sorts of missiles and large quantities of stones with great speed at the invading army. The soldiers will be knocked down and thrown into confusion.

HIPPOKRATES: The stories I have heard of your cleverness are true. You have contrived all sorts of war machines to use against our enemies. Let us prepare them for action at once.

(The two men leave immediately, for the invading forces will soon be upon Syracuse.)

Scene 2

The camp of Marcellus, just outside the walls of Syracuse. The Roman commander is conferring with his officers and engineers after a devastating attempt to besiege the city.

MARCELLUS: *(looking up at the walls of Syracuse)* We are certainly up against a formidable foe. All that I have heard of this Archimedes must be true. *(turning to his engineers)* How do his war machines work?

ROMAN LIEUTENANT: Some of my men think that they are fighting against the gods because many missiles are thrown at them so rapidly.

ROMAN ENGINEER: The machines have been contrived by a man who has studied mathematics extensively. Archimedes has made giant engines that are working models of geometry and mechanics. He uses levers and pulleys, cranks, cogwheels, and screws, as well as his knowledge of balance and the centers of gravity.

MARCELLUS: How are they powered?

ROMAN ENGINEER: By manpower, air power, and waterpower.

ROMAN LIEUTENANT: These war machines destroy our ships and kill our soldiers so effectively that my men become frightened whenever they see a rope or piece of wood projecting from the walls of the city. They run away shouting that another machine is appearing to kill them.

MARCELLUS: *(turning in jest to his own engineer)* Let us stop fighting this geometrical Briareus[3] who has destroyed our sambuca, treated our ships as if they were cups to ladle water from the sea, and hurled so many missiles against us, outdoing the hundred-handed monsters of mythology.

ROMAN LIEUTENANT: Look! Archimedes is aiming one of his engines at us. We must flee.

MARCELLUS: *(turning to his lieutenant)* I command that we end all fighting and assaults on the city and retreat to safety. Let us prepare for a long siege. But in the meantime, we shall attack and conquer other areas of Sicily that are held by the Carthaginians.

Syracuse remained unconquered for some time while Marcellus captured the ancient city of Megara; took the camp of Hippokrates at Acrillae, killing eight thousand men as they were building entrenchments; and overran much of Sicily. He was victorious everywhere he led his army.

---

3. Briareus was one of the three mythological Hekatoncheires, hundred-armed giants who were the sons of Uranos (Heaven) and Gaia (Earth).

Marcellus returned with the intention of blockading Syracuse by land and by sea. He came upon the city as the citizens were celebrating a festival in honor of the goddess Artemis. He noticed that a tower had been left poorly guarded and promptly had his men build ladders to scale the wall at night so as to take the city by surprise. At dawn, Marcellus ordered trumpets to sound, and the startled Syracusans fled in terror, thinking the entire city had been overrun by the Romans.

Syracuse was soon in Marcellus's possession. As he surveyed the beautiful city from a high point, Marcellus wept because he knew its impending fate. In those days, it was the custom for a conquering army to sack a defeated city. Marcellus could not prevent this, but he forbade the killing or enslaving of all free citizens. Marcellus was especially anxious to save the life of Archimedes, for whom he had developed much respect, and he immediately sent for him.

Scene 3

The house of Archimedes in Syracuse. The mathematician is concentrating so intently on a diagram he has drawn in glass dust that he has not heard the clamor created by the invading Romans, not even the blaring of trumpets. A soldier sent by Marcellus enters the house with orders to bring Archimedes to the Roman commander at once.

ROMAN SOLDIER: *(bursting into the house)* Is this the home of Archimedes? *(Archimedes ignores the soldier, his mind and eyes too involved with the problem he has drawn on the tray.)*

ROMAN SOLDIER: *(shouting)* Old man, are you Archimedes?

ARCHIMEDES: *(barely glancing up at the soldier)* Yes, I am Archimedes. Do not bother me.

ROMAN SOLDIER: I have orders to bring you to my commander, the Roman general Marcellus.

ARCHIMEDES: Leave me alone. I refuse to go anywhere until I solve this problem.

ROMAN SOLDIER: *(drawing his sword)* If you do not come with me, I will kill you at once!

ARCHIMEDES: Wait a moment. I do not want to leave my problem incomplete and unsolved. The wonders of science are more my concern than the affairs of generals.

Furious, the soldier kills the old man. When Marcellus finds out that Archimedes is dead, he has the soldier executed for murder. To pay tribute to the man he wished to meet, the Roman commander has the famous mathematician buried with much ceremony and also honors his friends and relatives.

During his lifetime, Archimedes had requested that upon his tomb there should be engraved the drawing of a cylinder circumscribing a sphere within it, together with an inscription giving the ratio of the cylinder to the sphere (3:2). He regarded his discovery of this ratio as his greatest accomplishment, more important than the invention of any war machine. Marcellus granted this wish as a tribute to the greatest mathematical genius of antiquity and possibly the greatest that the world has ever seen.

We're pretty smart for ancient folks!

A POTPOURRI OF CLASSICAL INGENUITY

Whereas the remains of a nation are monuments and buildings, the remains of a people are mostly houses and personal possessions. To understand past civilizations, we must study both types of remains. By doing so, we realize that the basic needs and wants of every civilization are the same. How a nation's people address these needs and wants is the measure of their ingenuity and creativity. Following is a sampling of how the ancients met some of their needs.

SALT AS A PRESERVING AGENT

Ancient Egyptian relief scenes and fish and other foods found intact in excavated tombs have taught us much about the methods used by ancient fishermen and cooks to preserve food. Salting was a favorite method of preservation, especially for fish, because the properties of salt hasten the drainage of body fluids and stop the deterioration of the meat.

The preservation process was as follows: The fish were gutted and/or slit from head to tail before being washed and hung on ropes to dry in the sun and wind. Coarse salt was rubbed on the fish before they were packed according to the following pattern: a layer of fish, a layer of salt, a layer of fish, a layer of salt. These bundles were covered and left for several days before being turned over and left for several more days. The finished product was a dry, hard fish whose tissues were permeated with salt.

TELEGRAPHY

Very early in human history, people learned to flash fire signals to members of other tribes. Through the centuries, many ingenious systems of telegraphy have been devised. Polybius, a second-century B.C. Greek historian, wrote about the system he invented:

MMM MMM GOOD!

130

– illustrated by Annette Cate

"Provide each tribe or participant with ten torches. Divide the torches into two groups of five each. Divide the twenty-four letters of the Greek alphabet into four groups of five letters and one group of four letters. Let the five torches in one group represent the five groups of Greek letters. Let each of the five torches in the other group represent a specific Greek letter from its group.

"To flash a message, have the person on duty use the following rules to spell out each word. First, raise the required number of torches in the first set of five to indicate the group to which a particular letter belongs. Then have him raise the required number of torches in the other set to indicate the specific letter within the group."

This system was accurate but tedious and required hours to spell out a message of considerable length.

DRY CLEANING

The ancients, especially the Egyptians and Romans, developed an effective dry-cleaning method that used water mixed with special herbs, plants, and urine. (The urine was collected in vessels placed on street corners and then allowed to decompose before it was used.)

First, the entire cloth was placed (or portions of it were dipped) into vessels containing the cleaning fluid. Then the cleaner used mallets and wooden sticks to beat the cloth. Roman wall paintings show cleaners using their hands and actually stepping into the vessels to pound the cloth with their feet. The wet, washed cloth was allowed to dry before being rinsed again in another solution and brushed with special tools made of teasel (a prickly plant), burs, thistles, or hedgehog prickles to raise the nap.

To bleach the cloth, the garment was placed over a wicker frame inside of which was a pan or pot

131

filled with burning sulfur. Since this process did not bleach evenly, the ancients rubbed the material with white or colored earth depending on the color of the cloth. Another brushing followed. Then the uneven fibers and threads were cut from the garment. Finally, the cloth was pressed between two boards worked with screws.

PUBLISHING

The invention of the printing press about A.D. 1440 signaled the end of the tedious recopying by hand of every letter of a book, text, speech, or law. But there had been a time, centuries earlier, when book publishing had gone at a relatively rapid pace.

During the first century B.C., the number of slaves in Rome grew rapidly. As conquest followed conquest, slaves were continually being sent to the city. Since many of them were well educated, they became teachers and professionals, although socially they remained slaves.

Educated Romans and others saw in these slaves a means to reprint great numbers of books, speeches, and decrees. The process was as follows: Up to one hundred educated slaves would sit in a room. A reader would stand before them and dictate a book, page by page. If more readers and several rooms were available, a book could be divided into sections. In a relatively short period of time, as many copies of the book as there were slaves would be ready for distribution.

REFRIGERATION

The Greeks and Romans dug large pits and covered them with grass, chaff, earth, manure, tree branches, and other substances that do not conduct heat. Then they collected snow from the mountains, pressed it together, and placed it inside the pit as a lining. Sometimes the snow was wrapped in thick cloths as a further measure against melting.

Hurry, man! This snow is COLD!

Ancient sources credit the Roman emperor Nero (A.D. 54–68) with inventing the "cooler." One day a shipment of produce packed in snow came to Rome from the north. Nero observed that the contents were quite cool as a result of having been next to the snow, not mixed with it. He applied the same principle to drinks. No longer did water and wine have to be mixed with snow to keep them cool. Now a glass or container filled with liquid had only to be placed in the snow to keep the contents cold.

PEDESTRIAN WALKWAYS

Modern crosswalks are marked in white at busy intersections. In addition, many intersections have lights regulating both vehicular and pedestrian traffic. Such concern for pedestrian safety is not new. As excavators removed volcanic debris from Pompeii, an Italian city south of Rome that was buried in the A.D. 79 eruption of Mount Vesuvius, they noticed sets of steppingstones along many streets. These stones allowed pedestrians to cross the street without having to maneuver around the ruts made by carriages and carts or to walk through animal excrement or waste products along the street.

Although steppingstones helped pedestrians avoid street litter and sewage, they did not prevent wheeled traffic, for the stones were spaced so that the wheels of carts, carriages, and chariots passed through the openings between them. To block a street off from vehicular traffic, stones high enough to prevent any wheeled vehicle from passing were placed along the street.

MAKE YOUR OWN SUNDIAL

You Need

very flat and level piece of
    wood or heavy cardboard
    measuring 5 by 5 inches
ruler
pencil
protractor
thin stick 3 inches long
pen or fine-tip marker

You could use a compass instead of a protractor!

Perhaps you have already made a simple sundial. On a sunny day, you may have drawn a circle in the sand or dirt, planted a stick in the middle, determined which direction was north, and then "read the shadow" of the stick to figure out the approximate time of day. For a more accurate reading, however, you first have to know the latitude of your location so that you can position your stick parallel to it. Then you need a protractor to measure the hours and a knife or sharp instrument to cut and mark the lines and numbers.

In this project, you will learn how to make a simple but quite useful type of sundial known as a meridian dial. A meridian dial does not show twelve o'clock noon because the rays of the sun are parallel to the face of the sundial at noon. The shadow that the gnomon (the scientific name for the stick) casts at noon is endless, and its edge cannot be seen.

Note: The time your meridian sundial is telling is solar time. However, the difference between mean solar time and clock time is never more than eighteen minutes, so your meridian sundial is quite accurate.

Aw, gee, mom, dad — it's not my fault I'm late! The stupid sundial wasn't working...

There was this big cloud...

– illustrated by Annette Cate

1. Smack-dab in the middle!

5 inches

1 inch

remember, you can also use a compass!

1. Mark the center of the wood or cardboard.

2. Using the center mark as your base, take the protractor and draw a circle with a 2-inch diameter (a 1-inch radius).

3. Draw a second circle 1/4 inch from the first circle (or a circle with a 2 1/2-inch diameter, or a 1 1/4-inch radius).

4. Draw a third circle 1/4 inch from the second circle (or a circle with a 3-inch diameter, or a 1 1/2-inch radius).

5. Draw a fourth circle 1/4 inch from the third circle (or a circle with a 3 1/2-inch diameter, or a 1 3/4-inch radius).

6. Place the stick in the center of the circles. Check to make sure the shadow cast by the stick is long enough to cross the four circles. (You need to take the board into the sun to check this.)

7. At 10 A.M., take your board outside to a specific spot. (You may choose any time you wish, but it must be a morning hour and the sun must be shining.) Look at the point where the shadow cast by the stick touches each of the circles.

Mark the spot on each circle.

8. At 3 P.M., take your board outside to the same spot you went to in the morning. (Again, you may choose any time you wish, but it must be an afternoon hour when the sun is shining.) Look at the point where the shadow cast by the stick touches each of the circles. Mark the spot on each circle.

9. Connect the pencil marks on each circle and find the exact middle point between the two marks.

10. With a pen, draw a line from the stick through all the middle points. Mark an N at the top of the fourth circle. This line, which intersects all four circles, is the meridian line, pointing due north to the celestial pole at the noon hour.

11. When you want to know the time, take your board outside to your spot. Look where the stick casts its shadow in relation to the line you drew pointing north. As the N represents both north and the noon hour, figure out the time of day in relation to the N. Good luck and have fun!

Here's the middle!

You'll get good at it with practice!

Kind of quiet to wake up to, though.

The good thing about the sun is that you never have to wind it!

And its batteries never go dead, either!

A CREATIVE MATCH

Match each clue with the inventor, invention, or phrase that it best describes. The answers can be found in the articles on the Greek inventors, pages 112–118, and on page 153.

1. Still used today by Egyptian farmers for irrigation. _____

2. A native of Alexandria. _____

3. Many of today's tools and machines are based on the use of these. _____

4. His specialty was creating amusing inventions. _____

5. This measures the distance a vehicle travels. _____

6. Its graduated scale compensated for shorter days in winter. _____

7. Archimedes shouted this when he solved the "gold crown" mystery. _____

8. He traveled to Alexandria to study. _____

a. Hero
b. Odometer
c. Archimedes
d. Water screw
e. *"Eureka! Eureka!"*
f. Ctesibius
g. Lever and fulcrum
h. Water clock

UNSCRAMBLE THE PEOPLE

Unscramble the jumbled words to determine the answers to the clues. Then place the numbered letters on the corresponding blank lines to discover whose preparations ensured Syracuse's freedom even after his death. The answers can be found in the play, pages 119–129, and on page 153.

1. He wanted to meet the great inventor of Syracuse.
sculrealm   _ _ _ _ _ _ _ _
                        4

2. They built the *sambuca* on the prows of their warships.
sonarm   _ _ _ _ _ _
                  5

3. His devotion to mathematics cost him his life.
damicshere   _ _ _ _ _ _ _ _ _ _
                         1

4. They wanted to defeat Rome for control of the Mediterranean Sea.
csinaaingrath   _ _ _ _ _ _ _ _ _ _ _ _ _
                                6

5. He committed murder to become the ruler of Carthage.
kphisorepat   _ _ _ _ _ _ _ _ _ _ _
                     2

6. He succeeded his father as ruler of Syracuse.
nogle   _ _ _ _ _
              3

His war preparations ensured Syracuse's freedom even after his death:

_ _ _ _ _ _
1 2 3 4 5 6

CROSSWORD PUZZLE

ACROSS

1. Used as a preserving agent
6. Made by carts in Roman roads
8. Ancient dry-cleaning ingredient
11. Used to work a clothes press
13. Erupted in A.D. 79
14. Ancient city buried by volcanic debris
15. Used to keep drinks cool
16. Used to make dry cleaners' brushing tools
17. Used to make dry cleaners' brushing tools
18. Greek who invented a system of telegraphy

DOWN

1. Ancient bleaching agent
2. Early Greeks used these to telegraph messages
3. Invented the "cooler"
4. Ancient dry cleaners used these to pound clothes
5. They commonly preserved fish
7. Roman "crosswalks"
9. Basic ingredient in ancient dry-cleaning fluid
10. Invented about A.D. 1440
12. Workers in ancient "publishing" houses

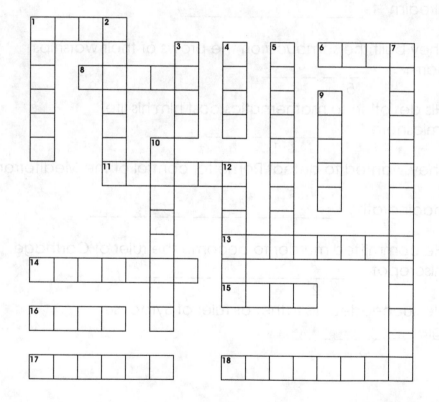

The answers can be found in the article on classical ingenuity, pages 130–133, and on page 153.

COMPANION

Topics for Comparison

1. Alexandria was one of the ancient world's intellectual capitals. What are today's intellectual capitals? Compare one or more of them with Alexandria. In your answer, include the prerequisites for being an intellectual capital, the type of people each attracts, and each one's location in relation to other intellectual centers.

2. How does Hero's steam engine compare with the modern-day whistling teakettle?

3. Compare Hero's odometer with car odometers and odometers that walkers strap to their ankles to measure the distance they travel.

4. How do today's irrigation systems compare with the water screw devised by Archimedes?

5. Compare Ctesibius's water organ with today's organ.

Suggestions for Writing Assignments

1. Expand on Hieron's argument that Archimedes owed it to Syracuse to develop military weapons to defend the city.

2. Part of Archimedes's success was the fear he instilled in the enemy. Did this fear contribute as much to Syracuse's independence as his machines? Comment and elaborate.

3. What do Marcellus's actions toward Syracuse and Archimedes tell you about the Roman general?

4. The sundial has its drawbacks, but so did the water clock. Can you name some problems with water clocks?

5. The ancient Roman pedestrian used steppingstones to cross the street. Do you think steppingstones could be used effectively today? If yes, where? If no, why not? Do you have any other suggestions for methods of ensuring pedestrian safety?

Further Activities

1. Take one or more of the inventions explained in this chapter and tell how you would improve its design.

2. Do some research on outboard motors and discover how their mechanism is based on Archimedes's water screw.

3. Make a simple lever and fulcrum (a seesaw or something similar in design). See how easily it allows you to move items in relation to its size.

4. Make a list of the tools and machines in your house and/or classroom that are based on the lever and fulcrum.

5. Experiment with the displacement of water. Take a two-cup measuring bowl. (You can use two measuring bowls if you have them.) Pour in one cup of water. Take two identical objects. Place one in the water. See how much the water level rises. Remove the object. (Be careful not to spill any water.) Place the other object in the water. Does it rise as much? It should if the two are identical. You can try this experiment using a great variety of objects and weights.

Topics for Debate

1. In a society based on slave labor or cheap labor, much time is wasted.

2. Overconfidence in machines and technology led to the Roman victory at Syracuse.

COMPANION Cross

Topics for Comparison

1. Greek artists stressed the beauty and magnificence of the human form; Roman artists stressed the power and strength of the individual. Compare and contrast how the two civilizations reflected this philosophical difference.

2. Compare and contrast Mausolos's and Hadrian's tombs. Include the reasons for the construction, the people involved, the subsequent uses of each tomb, and the sites today.

3. Compare and contrast Hadrian's Pantheon in Rome with the Parthenon in Greece.

4. Compare and contrast Rome's use of the arch and dome to create its engineering wonders with Greece's use of rectangular buildings to create its aesthetic wonders.

Suggestions for Writing Assignments

1. Massive, innovative building programs need patrons. Why? Compare the lives and motives of the patrons mentioned in this book.

2. Rome prided itself on its far-flung but unified empire. Greece was made up of separate city-states. Would a road system have helped Greece? If yes, was there any reason(s) Greece did not build one? If no, why not?

3. Today pollution and natural disasters are named the two culprits in the disintegration of many monuments. However, records show that humans have caused the destruction of many historical monuments. Which is worse? Or are they both equally bad?

4. Few people are acclaimed masters. This also was true in ancient times. Explain. You may use as examples masters in fields other than the arts and architecture, but you must tie your examples in with the masters mentioned in this book.

5. This book, and each chapter in it, begins with a quotation. Choose one quotation and explain its meaning in relation to the book or the chapter that it precedes. (Suggestion: Divide the class into six groups and assign each group one of the quotations.)

6. Greece's craftsmen reflected an emphasis on beauty and the excellence of the human body; Rome's craftsmen reflected an emphasis on power and conquest. What do you think future generations will say twentieth-century American craftsmen reflected? Explain your answer.

Further Activities

1. Find out whether any well-known architects, artists, sculptors, and/or inventors hail from your city, town, or state. Research their careers and works.

2. Ideas for collages:

   a. The works of Greek architects, sculptors, potters, and inventors

   b. The works of Roman architects, sculptors, and artists

   c. Modern-day buildings, statues, and vases crafted in the Greek style

   d. Modern-day buildings, statues, and paintings crafted in the Roman style

3. Host an art show using books, illustrations, drawings, and posters. The manner in which you set up your work could follow one of the following suggestions:

   a. Group by category, as the chapters in this book, and focus on the differences between the Greeks and Romans.

   b. Proceed chronologically beginning with the archaic Greek period and ending with the fall of Rome.

   c. Separate the Greek works from the Roman works and focus on each country.

Topics for Debate

1. It is wasteful to spend enormous amounts of money on monuments. They only crumble to ruins.

2. To be acclaimed an architectural or sculptural wonder, a work should be massive.

furtheREADING

1 THE SEVEN WONDERS OF THE ANCIENT WORLD

An Egyptian Pyramid by Jacqueline Morley, Mark Bergin, and John James (New York: Peter Bedrick Books, 1991) graphically depicts and explains the construction and uses of the pyramids while retelling how the ancient Egyptians lived and worked.

The Pyramid Explorer's Kit by Lee Horne (Philadelphia: Running Press, 1991) includes an excavation tool, labels, and step-by-step instructions for removing pieces of clay from a soft slab of rock so as to reconstruct the outline of Khufu's Great Pyramid.

The Seven Wonders of the Ancient World (1990), *The Seven Natural Wonders of the World* (1991), and *Seven Modern Wonders* (1992) by Celia King (San Francisco: Chronicle Books) are three miniature pop-up books featuring a colorful, creative illustration and brief historical account of each wonder.

Wonders of the World by Giovanni Caselli (New York: Dorling Kindersley, 1992) explains why and how each wonder was built. Each chapter opens with the artist's impression of the wonder. Comparisons between the wonders and similar later buildings also are included.

2 THE CLASSICAL TEMPLE

A Greek Temple by Fiona MacDonald and Mark Bergin (New York, Peter Bedrick Books, 1992) presents an illustrated survey of the construction and history of the Parthenon.

3 ANCIENT ARTISTS AND THEIR CRAFTS

A Greek Potter by Giovanni Caselli (New York: Peter Bedrick Books, 1992) describes the lifestyle and work habits of a fifth-century B.C. Athenian potter and his family.

Roman Art and Architecture by Mortimer Wheeler (London: Thames and Hudson, 1985) uses illustrations to discuss and explain the various aspects of Roman art in terms of its development in Italy and the rest of the Roman Empire.

4 ROME'S INGENIOUS ENGINEERS

City: A Story of Roman Planning and Construction by David Macaulay (Boston: Houghton Mifflin, 1974) uses text and black-and-white illustrations to show how the Romans planned and constructed their cities, aqueducts, roads, amphitheaters, bridges, temples, and houses.

The Magic Schoolbus at the Waterworks by Joanna Cole (New York: Scholastic, 1986) accompanies an innovative teacher who has her class experience firsthand the town's water-purification system.

GENERAL

The Archaeology of Greece: An Introduction (Ithaca, New York: Cornell University Press, 1980) is an excellent reference tool. It includes an overview of classical archaeology in Greece and descriptions and illustrations of the major monuments, sculptures, pottery, and paintings.

Architecture by Eleanor Van Zandt (Austin, Texas: Steck-

141

READING Further

Vaughn Company, 1990) provides a general history and overview of architecture from the Egyptian pyramids to contemporary forms.

Artists and Artisans by Irene M. Franck and David M. Brownstone (New York: Facts On File, 1987) traces the history of craft occupations such as painting, pottery making, sculpting, and glass blowing from early times to the twentieth century.

Builders by Irene M. Franck and David M. Brownstone (New York: Facts On File, 1985) tells of architects, road builders, construction workers, masons, and others from Egyptian times through the present.

Fun With Architecture by David Eisen (New York: Metropolitan Museum of Art and Viking, 1992) presents architecture's basic principles and includes stamps for readers to use to create innovative structures.

Greek Art and Archaeology by John Griffiths Pedley (New York: Harry N. Abrams, 1993) is an excellent introduction (for teachers) to the people whose culture and ideas gave birth to Western values. The clear and precise illustrations add considerably to a class presentation on the subject.

The Muses at Work: Arts, Crafts, and Professions in Ancient Greece and Rome edited by Carl Roebuck (Cambridge, Massachusetts: MIT Press, 1969) presents a collection of readable and informative essays about the artistic techniques used by the ancients. Diagrams and illustrations complement the text.

Start Exploring Architecture by Peter Dobrin (Philadelphia: Running Press Books, 1993) presents examples of architecture from around the world, both past and present. Accompanying black-and-white drawings give readers the opportunity to incorporate their own architectural ideas.

Then and Now by Stefania and Dominic Perring (New York: Macmillan, 1991) describes the wonders of the ancient world and the times in which they were built. Transparent see-through reconstructions allow readers to see the sites as they were and as they are today.

Amazing Buildings by Philip Wilinson, illustrated by Paolo Donati (New York: Dorling Kindersley, 1993) looks at the construction and decoration of twenty-one buildings from around the world, including the Colosseum and a sixteenth-century replica of an ancient Roman theater.

TEACHER'S guide

All the material presented in this book is geared to generating an interest in and an appreciation for the ancient artists, architects, and inventors of the Mediterranean world. Many of the pieces focus on the fact that the creative genius of the ancients continues to influence today's inventors, architects, and artists.

Chapter 1 introduces the Seven Wonders of the Ancient World, structures that inspired other ancients whose creations we now imitate. Chapters 2 and 4 focus on the architectural accomplishments of the ancient Greeks and Romans, while Chapter 3 features ancient artists and sculptors. All three chapters compare and contrast the two ancient cultures (Greece and Rome) and then explain how craftsmen in the Western world have imitated their predecessors. Chapter 5 focuses on the inventive genius of the Greeks.

The overview at the beginning of each chapter provides a steppingstone to the material contained within. Classroom units and integrated arts units can be built using the overview as the base. In fact, each chapter can be treated as a complete unit and studied individually throughout a semester or the school year. The Cross Companion could be used as the final unit.

Each chapter contains a series of puzzles that will test students' retention of the material presented. The answers to all the puzzles are presented in the Teacher's Guide.

To encourage students to see the relationships and contrasts between the past and the present, and between Greece and Rome, we have included a Companion section at the end of each chapter. This section is designed to involve students mentally and physically in understanding and developing the thoughts and ideas presented in the chapter. The Cross Companion should be used to encourage students to compare, contrast, and evaluate what they have read and observed in all the preceding chapters.

Many of the Further Activities could be treated as interdisciplinary topics, and classes and/or individual students could work on them in the science or language arts classroom as well as the social studies classroom. Such cooperative efforts would help students see that interrelationships between the various disciplines exist at all levels.

Most Companion questions do not have definite right or wrong answers. Students are asked to become critical thinkers, not just repeaters of what they have read. Therefore, you will not find a suggested answer for every question in the Teacher's Guide. Rather this guide offers, whenever appropriate, additional information to help teachers evaluate students' responses. The Topics for Debate are not referred to in the guide, as the arguments for each of the opposing sentiments will vary widely among students. The basic arguments for each side are obvious.

A note on spelling: We have followed the Greek spelling in the transliteration of Greek names and the Latin spelling in the transliteration of Roman names. For example, Halikarnassos is spelled with a *k* and an *os* as it would have been by the Greeks. Its Latin equivalent is Halicarnassus. Exceptions: We chose to keep the *c* in Acropolis, Crete, Corinth, and Pericles and the *c* and *us* in Croesus to conform to the present-day English spelling of these names.

ANSWERS

Crossword Puzzle

Across: 2. Chares, **5.** tomb, **7.** Lapiths, **10.** Nile, **11.** Goths, **15.** red, **16.** *faros*, **17.** Diodoros, **18.** blue, **21.** Peloponnesos, **23.** three, **25.** A.D., **26.** horses, **28.** Zeus, **30.** Asia Minor, **31.** bronze, **32.** two, **33.** Deinokrates, **35.** zoo, **36.** Elis, **37.** pharaohs, **38.** Karia.

Down: 1. Nike, **3.** Helios, **4.** Skopas, **6.** walls, **7.** limestone, **8.** Herodotos, **9.** *pharus*, **12.** stones, **13.** Nebuchadrezzar, **14.** marble, **19.** earthquake, **20.** gold, **21.** Pausanias, **22.** Sostrates, **24.** Egypt, **27.** Ptolemy, **29.** Rome, **34.** oil.

Philon's Sites and Sights

1. d., **2.** f., **3.** e., **4.** b., **5.** g., **6.** a., **7.** c.

A Common Neighbor

1. Mausolos, **2.** Aegean Sea, **3.** cedar, **4.** Christianity, **5.** lighthouse, **6.** Greece, **7.** worm borers, **8.** Alexandria, **9.** Artemisia, **10.** Constantinople, **11.** Olympic Games, **12.** Croesus, Lydia, **13.** Hanging Gardens, **14.** Skopas, Timotheos, **15.** chryselephantine, **16.** Deinokrates, Leochares. A common neighbor: Mediterranean Sea.

Topics for Comparison

1. Answers should include the reasons for construction; the historical circumstances under which each was built; the construction materials used; whether the projects were built for public or private purposes; which still stand today and the purpose each serves; the cause of destruction of those that no longer exist.
2. Answers may include remodeling of old factories to house malls, restaurants, and other businesses; reuse of old fireplaces, mantels, and marble in new buildings; remaking of closed military bases and malls into schools and housing for the elderly.
3. The Taj Mahal, located on the southern bank of the Yamuna River outside the city of Agra in India, was begun in 1632 and took approximately twenty-two years to complete. It was built by the Mughal emperor Shah Jahan of India as a mausoleum for his wife, Arjumand Banu Begam, who had died in childbirth in 1631. Comparisons may be made on the basis of size, number of workers, style of architecture, and setting.
4. Comparisons should include title or office held by the deceased; honorable deeds performed by the deceased; person or persons responsible for erecting the monument; purpose of the monument; style used.
5. Three of the basic reasons are the prohibitive cost, the shortage of workers needed to accomplish such a time-consuming task, and the lack of skilled workmanship.
6. The Space Needle in Seattle, Washington, the Empire State Building in New York City, and the Prudential Building in Boston are three examples. Revolving restaurants atop buildings also can be given as examples.

Suggestions for Writing Assignments

1. Wonders are chosen because of the magnificence of the building design, the purpose of the building, and the ingenuity that fostered such a creation. Students may add their own reasons, but they should be very specific and detailed. Comparisons can be made between ancient and modern wonders. The issue of whether the criteria for wonders are the same today as they were in ancient times also may be addressed.
4. Students should note that

ANSWERS

although a civilization may not be at its peak when a wonder is created, the fortunes of the reigning king or government must be high. Checking into the fortunes of the commissioner of each wonder also would make for an interesting paper.

5. The construction materials used reflect the area where the structure is located. If the people are very prosperous, they can afford imported materials. War does not preclude building efforts, but it certainly reduces the avail-ability of a large work force. Climate definitely has an effect on building, as an area with more sun and temperate weather allows builders to spend more time on a particular project. However, with the pyramids, the three-month shifts certainly produced wonders.

6. A monument that is recognized as magnificent gives the builders a sense of pride. The natives of the area feel this same sense of pride, especially as visitors flock to the area, remarking on the ingenuity of the monument's creators.

Further Activities

4. The seven natural wonders are the Great Barrier Reef in Australia, the caves in the Pyrenees mountains separating Spain and France, the harbor at Rio de Janeiro in Brazil, the Paricutín Volcano in Mexico, the Grand Canyon in the United States, Victoria Falls in Africa, and Mount Everest in the Himalayas. Most are millions of years old. All are natural phenomena created by the continually changing forces of our planet.

5. The basic tale says that Oenomaos, the king of Elis, promised his daughter Hippodamia to the person who defeated her in a foot-race. Pelops did so, and to commemorate his victory, he instituted the Olympic Games.

6. Pirithoos was the king of the Lapiths, a mythical people who inhabited the mountains of Thessaly in northern Greece. Because of his father Ixion's indiscretions, he had half-brothers called Centaurs. Pirithoos was able to arrange a peaceful agreement with the Centaurs. However, at Pirithoos's wedding, the Centaurs drank too much wine and attempted to seize Pirithoos's bride. A struggle ensued, and the Lapiths, with the help of the legendary Greek king Theseus, defeated the Centaurs. Pirithoos then made an agreement with Theseus to capture and marry one of Zeus's daughters. Theseus took Helen (the same Helen who was taken to Troy), only to lose her when her brothers freed her. Pirithoos was then determined to steal Persephone. Pirithoos and Theseus ventured into the underworld, where Hades, the king of the underworld, seized them. Another Greek hero, Herakles, was allowed to free Theseus but not Pirithoos.

ANSWERS

A Jumbled Fortress

Acropolis; Athena; Athens, Sparta; Parthenon, Propylaia; Erichthonios, Kekrops; Iktinos, Kallikrates; karyatides; mosque; *naos*; Nike; Peloponnesian; Pericles; Persians; Pheidias; Plataiai, Salamis; *polis*.

Greek Temple Scramble

1. Ionic, 2. architrave, 3. dowels, 4. stylobate, 5. acanthus, 6. *antefixa*, 7. Doric, 8. pediment, 9. stereobate, 10. metopes. The Greek name for the temple chamber where the offerings of worshipers were placed: *opisthodomos*.

Greece Versus Rome:

1. f, 2. d, 3. a, 4. g, 5. b, 6. h, 7. c, 8. j, 9. e, 10. i.

Topics for Comparison

1. Answer should include the following: The dome and vault created more interior space and produced a feeling of grandeur. Because the dome covered a circular space, it allowed light to reach every section, eliminating the dark corners created when using a square or rectangular design. The use of the arch in structures such as aqueducts lent a more graceful appearance to the structure than a post-and-lintel style would have. There could be arches of various sizes within the same building, a variation impossible within the confines of the post-and-lintel design. However, the arch, dome, and vault also can result in structures without aesthetic appeal because of their enormous size. The post-and-lintel style, though simple and practical, conveys an impression of strength and solidarity.

2. Known to history as Lord Elgin, Thomas Bruce (1766–1841) was the seventh Earl of Elgin and a British diplomat and art collector. From 1799 to 1803, Elgin held the post of British ambassador to the Ottoman Empire in Constantinople. Aware that the Acropolis was in disrepair and fearing for its preservation, Elgin petitioned the Turkish authorities to take "pieces of stone with old inscriptions or figures" back to England. Permission was granted, and Elgin immediately began packing and shipping the treasures to England. They included friezes, pediment sculptures, and fragments of statues from the Parthenon and a column, capital, architrave, cornice, and karyatid from the Erechtheion. Elgin also shipped artifacts from other ancient Greek sites to England.

Suggestions for Writing Assignments

1. Thomas Jefferson had a sound classical education beginning in grammar school. In 1784, he traveled to France, where he spent considerable time reading, visiting museums, and engaging in discussions with the intellectuals of Paris. Jefferson was keenly interested in architecture and favored the classical style. Because of the offices he held and the fact that he was well respected throughout the United States, Jefferson's ideas on architecture were widely known and followed. In 1785, he planned the state capitol in Richmond, Virginia, with the help of a Frenchman named Charles-Louis Clérisseau. This was the first public building in modern times based on the design of an ancient temple. Jefferson incorporated the plan of a Roman villa into the design of his home, Monticello, in Virginia. Always a proponent of education, Jefferson established the University of

146

Virginia. By using the classical style for its buildings, he attempted to educate the citizenry as to the beauty and simplicity of this style of architecture. Jefferson felt that the values of the new United States could best be symbolized through architecture.

2. Background information: Throughout its history, Athens paid special homage to its patron goddess, Athena, a fact reflected in the temples of the Acropolis. After the Greeks defeated the Persians, Athens assumed a leading role in Greek politics. The pride its citizens and leaders felt allowed them to put enormous energy into a building program. Athens grew ever more prosperous. The arts, literature, and building programs flourished. Peace allowed artisans to concentrate on extras rather than just the essential needs of a war-torn or struggling community. After Athens's defeat in the Peloponnesian War, the Athenians turned inward and questioned their leadership role in the Greek peninsula. Economic and personal hardships did not allow the Athenians to spend time and energy on restoring war-damaged and neglected buildings, much less on conceiving new projects. For centuries, Greece came under foreign domination: Alexander the Great, the Romans, and later the Ottomans. Artistic genius and building programs are difficult to accomplish when a nation is subservient to another. The Greeks won independence from Ottoman rule in 1830, but the ensuing governments were somewhat unstable. Since 1973, a democratically elected government has presided over the country. As a result, the Athenians and the Greek government have supported and continue to support laws that will minimize the possibility of damage to the Acropolis. Also, many restoration projects are in progress. (Refer to the project mentioned in "The Ravages of Time," page 39.)

3. The British-born architect Benjamin Latrobe (1764–1820) is considered the first professional architect in the United States. In 1803, Thomas Jefferson appointed him surveyor of public buildings. He designed the Bank of Pennsylvania in Philadelphia, considered the first monument to the Greek Revival movement in America.

Latrobe also was in charge of completing the Capitol Building in Washington, D.C. He is best known for the Basilica of the Assumption of the Blessed Virgin Mary in Baltimore, Maryland. Charles Bulfinch (1763–1844) is considered the first professional "American" architect in the United States. When in Paris, Jefferson advised Bulfinch to study the designs of the major buildings throughout France and Italy. Bulfinch designed the Massachusetts State House in Boston, the Connecticut State House in Hartford, and the Maine Capitol in Augusta. He followed Latrobe as the American architect of the U.S. Capitol Building. Other Greek Revival architects were William Strickland (1788–1854), whose works include the Athenaeum in Providence, Rhode Island, and the Masonic Temple, the U.S. Mint, and the U.S. Custom House in Philadelphia; Thomas Walter (1804–1887), whose works include Founders Hall at Girard College in Philadelphia and Andalusia, the home of Nicholas Biddle (financier and scholar) near Philadelphia.

4. During the Middle Ages,

the works and values of the ancient Greeks and Romans were ignored. The Renaissance, with its emphasis on the value of the individual and on learning, saw an intense interest in studying the classics. The arts were promoted, and sculptors, architects, and artists began studying the Greek and Roman works that had survived. A renewed appreciation for the genius of past civilizations followed, as did a desire to copy and emulate what the ancients had accomplished. When the United States won its independence from England, it wanted to show that it was independent in every way. No longer did architects want to copy only English styles. They went to Italy and France to study the many buildings that were being modeled after those remaining from classical times. This was perfect for the young United States. Greece, with its democratic government and hard-won freedom from the Persians, and Rome, one of the greatest empires that ever existed, were considered worthy models.

5. Citizens considered these buildings the barometer of a state's or a nation's power and affluence. The Greek Revival style was believed to be the perfect style to provide a sense of independence, freedom, power, and potential prosperity. Examples exist in every state (college campuses, federal buildings, state supreme courts), but it is a good idea to select local examples to which students can relate. The federal buildings in Washington, D.C., with which most students are familiar, also can be included.

6. Examples are the British Museum in London, the Brandenburg Gate in Berlin (this was inspired by the Propylaia), the Church of the Madeleine in Paris, and the Prado Museum in Madrid.

Further Activities

4. Fifth-century B.C. Athens was the principal Greek city-state, and its navy commanded the eastern Mediterranean Sea. Athens's tributary states each paid a tax, adding to Athens's wealth. Athens was shifting gradually from a monarchy to a democracy. It was becoming the art center of the world. Fifth-century B.C. personalities were the dramatists Sophokles and Euripides, the comic poet Aristophanes, the historian Herodotos, the philosopher Sokrates, and the sculptors Pheidias, Myron, and Polykleitos.

A Greek and Roman Match

1. d, 2. g, 3. f, 4. i, 5. a, 6. c, 7. j, 8. b, 9. e, 10. h.

Crossword Puzzle

Across: 1. Aristotle, **4.** Polygnotos, **6.** wood, **7.** landscape, **11.** Herculaneum, **13.** fresco, **14.** Ionian, **17.** Zeuxis, **18.** Mediterranean, **21.** portraiture, **23.** Romans, **24.** Pompeii, **25.** marketplace.
Down: 2. sponge, **3.** encaustic, **4.** Parrhasios, **5.** linen, **8.** architectural, **9.** wax candle, **10.** doors, **12.** mortar, **15.** Aegean, **16.** Vergina, **19.** sponge, **20.** fifth, **22.** four.

A Potter's Scramble

1. gourds, 2. clay, 3. kiln, 4. firing, 5. gray-black, 6. buff-red, 7. spy hole, 8. chimney. The name given to the style of vases made by early Greek potters: black-figured.

Topics for Comparison

1. Answer should include the following: The Romans stressed realism in portraiture. The Greeks stressed beauty and simplicity. For the Greeks, this simplicity and beauty could best be expressed by representing nature as realistically as possible. A Roman artist would probably have added some decorative designs to the curtain and/or cord, and certainly to the grapes and table. Greek artists followed the rule that realism was simplicity in design.

2. The Greeks were more introspective and religious than the Romans. As a result, their works of art, regardless of the age, reflected this. The Greeks felt that the gods should be thanked and honored for creating such a superb piece of workmanship as the human body. The individual personality did not matter as much as the body, which allowed a person to accomplish great deeds. Unnecessary details weakened an artist's composition. Power and might provided the Greek artist with the atmosphere to create works of art reflecting this philosophy of life. In contrast, the Romans honored the individual, not his or her form. They placed importance on what an individual did that made him or her different or greater than anyone else. Not as religious as the Greeks, Roman artists sought to have their creations reflect the power and accomplishments of their leaders. Unnecessary additions were further examples of their need to show their worth in material terms.

3. To a Greek, the delineation of the body's form was the most important part of the statue. The action and power of the body's muscles, the various positions it could assume, and the tautness of the muscles were important to the Greeks. Greek works of art were more symbolic than individually realistic. The Roman artist wanted to make sure the observer of a statue knew exactly whom the statue represented. The Roman eye was trained to look for the personality. Therefore, the body was not of great importance.

4. As Rome's might grew and more provinces were added, the decorations on the interior walls of Roman buildings changed. The First Style was simple: no vistas or grand ideas. Lines sometimes broke the monotony of a plain color. As the houses grew in size and Rome's outlook seemed more prosperous, pictures and scenes were added (Second Style). Romans also were beginning to accumulate money, which allowed them to

ANSWERS

take vacations and buy second homes in the country or near the shore. Prosperity gave Romans more leisure time. Resorts cropped up. Landscape scenes and people enjoying such areas were great backdrops for a room, especially a vacation home or a room in a primary residence whose owners also had a second home (Third Style). The Fourth Style seemed to include everything. It was fantastic, resembling a scene from the theater.

5. Washington has more than three hundred memorials and statues, including the Lincoln Memorial, the Jefferson Memorial, the Theodore Roosevelt Memorial, the Washington Monument, statues commemorating Civil War heroes, memorial benches, temple-style buildings, and the Vietnam War Memorial.

Suggestions for Writing Assignments

1. The archaic forms of Greek sculpture reflect Greece's emergence as a nation. Beneath the stylized, draped cloth is a knee and leg tentatively attempting to break out of its confining restrictions. Aware of its ability to repel invaders, Greece gained a self-

confidence that provided artists with a climate in which to experiment and visually reproduce the bodies of its citizens—the people whom the gods had endowed with the ability to use every muscle for the good and glory of Greece. In Athens, the champion of Greek liberty, the democratic form of government created a political and philosophical atmosphere that stimulated creativity. As Greece began to decline, the confidence of Greek artists also began to decrease. When conquering nations marveled at the works of the old masters, Greek artists sought identity and self-worth in copying their predecessors' works.

2. After a military victory, people throughout history have often felt the need to destroy or remove anything that symbolizes or represents the people they have just defeated. The reasons for this desire have been the subject of study for psychologists, many of whom feel this behavior is often cathartic. There are many examples: the storming of the Bastille during the French Revolution, the execution of Mussolini, and the trials of the Nazi war criminals.

5. The Greeks believed that simplicity expressed beauty. Answers could include examples from everyday life.

6. Examples are the 1939 statue of Theodore Roosevelt (in front of the American Museum of Natural History in New York City), the 1915 statue of Joan of Arc (Ninety-third Street and Riverside Drive in New York City), and the Cecil Rhodes Memorial at Groote Schuur in Cape Town, South Africa.

A Wet Scramble

1. Appia, Marcia, 2. Apennines, 3. Augustus, 4. reservoir, 5. travertine, 6. *castellum aquarum,* 7. Frontinus, 8. pozzolana, 9. terra cotta, 10. Tiber. Romans had these to collect household water: *castella privata.*

A Colossal Puzzle

1. *velarium,* 2. *venationes,* 3. masts, 4. chapels, 5. *naumachiae,* 6. *kolossos,* 7. pollution, 8. Flavian Amphitheater, 9. travertine. Emperor responsible for construction of Colosseum: Vespasian.

A Wordy Fortress

Aelian; angel; Antoninus Pius; Apollo; Aurelian; cypress; drum; dungeons; Italy; marble; mausoleum; mosaics; museum; Ostrogoths; peperino, travertine; pilaster; Theodoric; Tiber; Vatican; Visigoths; white.

Topics for Comparison

1. Answers should include the following: our system of highway signs on archways above roads and to the left and right of roads; the Romans' use of stone markers and the central milestone in Rome. Students need to use road maps and encyclopedia maps of Rome's roads. Historically, the frontiersmen and pioneers carved out the first roads in the United States as they sought new land. A central road system for communication and commercial purposes followed. Rome's roads followed its conquests, first of Italy and then of the Mediterranean world. For Rome, communication and the ability to deploy troops quickly to a "hot spot" were important. Troops often constructed or supervised the construction of roads in the provinces.

2. The project in this chapter could be a starting point for this question. Students also could contact the state's department of public works about road construction and current road projects in the area. Answers should include materials used, depth of the foundation, width of the road, drainage systems, use or lack of stop signs and the like, and repair schedules.

3. Research also is needed for this answer. Each student (a class could be divided into groups) could be assigned a specific aspect of the U.S. or city water system to research. Information can be gathered in the library and by calling or visiting the local water department. Emphasis could be placed on the purification of water today. A visit to sites where waste and water are treated would provide material for students to continue a discussion in class. This question also could be done in cooperation with the students' science teacher.

4. Students can choose a specific sports stadium in the United States. If the student wishes to do further research, or if the class is divided into groups, a comparison between small arenas used in Roman towns and the stadium in the students' city or hometown would be interesting. Another possibility is a comparison between small stadia and stadia where professional games are played.

5. The purpose of Hadrian's mausoleum was to house the corpse of an emperor, and its use continued as such, albeit for a short period of time. Arlington National Cemetery was originally (in the early 1800s) the estate of George Washington's adopted son. During the Civil War, northern troops occupied the land, and in 1864 the U.S. secretary of war declared it a national

ANSWERS

cemetery. War dead from every war have been buried at Arlington. Outstanding leaders such as Robert E. Peary and Robert F. Kennedy also are buried there.

Suggestions for Writing Assignments

1. Lead was commonly used for pipes and dishes. It has been noted that only the well-to-do could afford lead dishes and that the poor used earthenware or clay dishes. Hence, some historians have proposed the theory that the lead in the pipes and dishes contributed to the fact that there were so many mentally unbalanced Roman leaders in the later years of the empire. Students could find out the effects of lead poisoning that are known today and the laws against the use of lead paint in their state. This project could be done in cooperation with the students' science teacher.

2. Hadrian was the Roman emperor responsible for unifying and consolidating the empire. He traveled extensively throughout the provinces. Have students use illustrated books that show Hadrian's mausoleum, Pantheon, and villa. Have them reflect on his admiration for and use of the Greek style of architecture. These structures have become symbols of the days when Rome ruled the Mediterranean world. They draw millions of tourists to Rome.

3. Rome extended its road system wherever it wanted to extend its power. Roads kept military outposts in touch with each other and with Rome.

Further Activities

3. Two of the most famous aqueducts still standing today are the Pont du Gard near Nîmes, France, and the aqueduct in Segovia, Spain.

ANSWERS 5

A Creative Match

1. d, **2.** f, **3.** g, **4.** a, **5.** b, **6.** h, **7.** e, **8.** c.

Unscramble the People

1. Marcellus, **2.** Romans, **3.** Archimedes, **4.** Carthaginians, **5.** Hippokrates, **6.** Gelon. His war preparations ensured Syracuse's freedom even after his death: Hieron.

Crossword Puzzle

Across: 1. salt, **6.** ruts, **8.** urine, **11.** screws, **13.** Vesuvius, **14.** Pompeii, **15.** snow, **16.** burs, **17.** teasel, **18.** Polybius.
Down: 1. sulfur, **2.** torches, **3.** Nero, **4.** feet, **5.** Egyptians, **7.** steppingstones, **9.** water, **10.** printing, **12.** slaves.

Topics for Comparison

1. A list of intellectual capitals might include Boston, Paris, London, and Tokyo. Included in the prerequisites should be schools located in the area; research centers; world-famous scientists, physicians, and artists; cultural centers; and museums.
2–5. These questions require students to use the library to find illustrations and explanations.

Suggestions for Writing Assignments

1. Answers may include the following arguments: Whether Archimedes designed war machines or not, Syracuse would be attacked. If Syracuse lost, its citizens also would lose. To keep Syracuse and its citizens free, a victory was necessary. Archimedes could design weapons that would wreak havoc with the enemy's strategy and tire and frustrate the enemy, not weapons aimed at total destruction. Perhaps the principles involved in the design of the war machines could later be used in peacetime.
2. Answers may include the following arguments: Continued fear creates suspense, which in turn can cause panic and lead to retreat and defeat. Fear of the unknown is common to everyone. Archimedes's foes did not know or understand his inventions. Because they seemed unexplainable, they caused fear.
3. Marcellus does not appear to be bloodthirsty or vengeful. His goal was conquest. Once Syracuse was his, the destruction would be aimed against what he then controlled. His treatment of Archimedes's family and the inhabitants of Syracuse illustrates a respect for life and the powers of the intellect.
4. Answers could include the following: Even the smallest pinprick of a hole could cause loss of water; freezing temperatures could cause water to freeze; the water clock was cumbersome; water clocks needed constant attention.

153

Cross ANSWERS Companion

Topics for Comparison

1–4. Students' answers should be based on research using history books, encyclopedias, maps, and architectural illustrations.

Suggestions for Writing Assignments

1. The two patrons mentioned are Pericles and Hadrian. Their drive, energy, and willingness to allocate funds contributed to the success of their building programs.

2. Ancient Greece's system of individually ruled city-states did not create a need for a massive road system. Various mountain ridges divide Greece, the Gulf of Corinth separates southern Greece from the north, and the fingerlike land formations of the Peloponnesos meant further isolation in the southern Greek communities. In addition, Greece's colonies in Asia Minor and southern Italy could be reached faster by water than by land. Under these circumstances, a fleet of ships was more important than a road system. Students also should research the road system used in Greece today.

3. Students should check the reasons for the destruction of each monument they include in their answers. If both humans and natural disasters have affected a monument, students can explain which did the most damage or the most irreparable damage.

4. Perhaps to make this more relevant to students, you should encourage them to look at acclaimed masters in a field in which they are interested.

154

INDEX

INDEX

Charles F. Baker and Rosalie F. Baker are the founders and editors of the magazine *CALLIOPE: World History for Young People.* Together they have written two books, *The Classical Companion* and *Myths and Legends of Mount Olympos.* Mr. Baker also is the author of *The Struggle for Freedom,* a series of plays on the American Revolution. Both have served as teachers and administrators in public and private schools.